Dedicated to my wife, Joyce, who supports me in all my creative endeavors

REFLECTIONS ON COMPOSING

Four American Composers

ELWELL SHEPHERD ROGERS COWELL

with four portraits by George Mauersberger

Frederick Koch

Carnegie-Mellon University Press

Carnegie-Mellon University Press
Pittsburgh Pennsylvania

ISBN 0-915604-20-5
LC 78-59839

Printed and bound in the United States of America

CONTENTS

Permission is granted from Fema Music Publishing Company, of Chicago, for the quotations from *Three Poems* of Robert Liddell Lowe by Herbert Elwell; from Theodore Presser Company to quote from the *Triptych* for High Voice and String Quartet of Arthur Shepherd, and also to reproduce excerpts from *Three Japanese Dances* by Bernard Rogers; and permission from Associated Music Publishers of New York to quote from the piano piece *Tiger* by Henry Cowell. Permission is also granted by the Plain Dealer to reproduce music reviews by Herbert Elwell and by the Cleveland Press to reproduce reviews by Arthur Shepherd.

FOREWORD

It is always heart-warming to come upon a genuine labor of love. Such is Frederick Koch's tribute to four American composers with whom he had the good fortune to study at various stages in the course of his career as pianist, composer and teacher. Teaching is arduous business, and writing music is even more so; we are indebted to the author not only for illuminating both facets of the professional lives of four significant figures in American music, but also for providing us with vignettes that richly underscore the humanity of these men.

Many, if not most, composers in the twentieth century have also been teachers. In many instances this is so because the composers freely chose to be teachers as well. While I do not believe for one minute that any composer ever really believed that the art of composition was something that could actually be taught in the way that mathematics, for example, is taught, I nevertheless feel that composers tend to bring to their teaching activities and hence pass on to their students something of their own creative outlook that illumines the art of music in a very special way. This was certainly the case with the four men about whom Frederick Koch has written.

It was my privilege to have known and worked with Bernard Rogers, as a student in his composition class and later as a colleague on the faculty of the Eastman School of Music. I cannot refrain from acknowledging a debt to him that can be repaid in only one way that I know of, by passing along to another generation of students something of his enthusiasm for the art of music and his spirit of humility as a creative artist.

In a real sense a great teacher reveals himself in his teaching, and this was certainly true not only of Rogers, but also of Herbert Elwell, Arthur Shepherd and Henry Cowell. I had only the briefest of contact with Shepherd, but I have fond memories of working with both Elwell and Cowell during a number of summer sessions at the Eastman School. The students of all these men were exceedingly fortunate; for they came away, if they were at all perceptive, with both a reverence for music as an art and a profound awareness of the difficulty as well as the rewards of writing it.

Through his class notes Frederick Koch is able to share his insights into the artistic personalities of the four composers; and he further provides us with an understanding look at some of their actual music. Especially valuable are the lists of compositions provided for each composer. His most useful service, however, is in capturing something of the distilled wisdom of men who loved to teach as well as write, and who contributed significantly as teachers to the development of American music through their contact with several generations of students.

Wayne Barlow
Rochester, New York

INTRODUCTION

Beginning in the early twentieth century America felt the influence of such important European composers as Bartok, Stravinsky, Schoenberg and Hindemith. The eminence of such distinguished Europeans has been to strengthen the image of the composer as professor in the eyes of the public and to convince university administrators and policy makers of the legitimacy of music composition as a part of the academic curriculum.

Heretofore many composers from the United States went to France to join the classes of the great teacher Nadia Boulanger, who lists among her students Aaron Copland, Elliott Carter, Douglas Moore, Roy Harris, Walter Piston, Virgil Thompson, Quincy Porter, Herbert Elwell and many others. Universities soon began to bring composers in residence to their campuses, which led to festivals of contemporary music and to the development of an American school of composers. Whereas in the 1920's it seemed necessary for a budding composer to travel to Europe for the stamp of approval, today it is possible to study with outstanding teachers here in this country.

A school of composers grew up in the 1920's in Cleveland, under the leadership of Ernest Bloch, who at that time headed the Cleveland Institute of Music. This group included Roger Sessions, Arthur Shepherd, Herbert Elwell, Quincy Porter and later, Beryl Rubinstein. The writer felt himself fortunate in having two of these composers as teachers: Herbert Elwell and Arthur Shepherd.

Herbert Elwell was well known for his thought-provoking Sunday columns in the *Plain Dealer* and for his astute reviews as music critic. In addition he is heralded today as one of the finest composers of art songs and compositions for voice and orchestra and as a teacher extraordinaire.

Arthur Shepherd was assistant conductor of the Cleveland Orchestra, program annotator for the program books of the orchestra, music critic for the *Cleveland Press,* Chairman of the Music Department of Western Reserve University, chamber music pianist, active composer and dedicated teacher.

At the same time of this flourishing of creative activity in Cleveland there was another center developing in Rochester, where Dr. Howard Hanson, Director of the Eastman School of Music, had as a member of his faculty Bernard Rogers, who had studied with Ernest Bloch in Cleveland.

Bernard Rogers was a superb orchestrator and composer, an inspired teacher, and the author of an important text *The Art of Orchestration.* Howard Hanson innovated a series of American Music Festivals and made recordings of many American composers' works in Rochester which brought about a healthy interest in American music and in the people writing it.

Henry Cowell, who grew up in California and was practically self-taught, has been one of the important innovators of the twentieth century. He served on the faculties of Columbia University, the New School of Social Research and for a number of years on the faculty of the Eastman School of Music during the summer sessions. His book *New Musical Resources* recently reprinted by Something Else Press is now a significant source of reference for the avant garde.

The experience of working with these men through the 50's and 60's was a most worthwhile one for it brought me into contact with their varied backgrounds and different outlooks on music. Both were stimulating and refreshing.

Since World War II, a gap developed between those composers who proclaimed their abandonment and disengagement from history, and those who reassessed the value and necessity of historical continuity. Today in the freedom of the arts, originality, the personal statement, and experimentation are mandatory. Appollonaire wrote: 'The poet has surprised you and he will surprise you again. It is he who discusses new joys even if they are hard to bear.' The late Henry Cowell said, 'No single inherited style or single acquired technique will enable a composer to live in the twentieth century.'

The tendency is to ignore what has happened in the past as music becomes more controlled in every aspect even to the doing away with the performer, as witnessed in electronic and computor composed compositions. Sometimes it is completely uncontrolled, as in the aleatoric or so-called 'happenings.' One well-known composer when asked what he was trying to communicate said, 'I don't know — I leave that to Western Union.'

Today it may be difficult for even two composers to talk with one another depending upon which side of the fence they happen to be. I see no reason for the musician of today with perhaps a conservative outlook to feel pushed aside for the small coterie of the avant garde.

To maintain order there must be peaceful coexistence. I believe that it is possible for all composers, regardless of viewpoint, to live side by side working together to create music of our century that will live. Music with a sense of humor, with hope, love and faith that transcends these troubled times is needed today.

We can learn from each other and it is for this reason that I have chosen to relate some class room discussions on composing with these four outstanding American composers. Today they may be considered conservative and their views not quite as relevant to contemporary thought, but they were forward thinking and have contributed much to the advancement of American music in this century. The work of all four men is representative of the best on the American scene. It exhibits craft as well as inspired musical ideas that are progressive and remain vital and expressive.

Frederick Koch

I wish to acknowledge the following for their assistance in the preparation of this book—Mrs Arthur Shepherd, Mrs Bernard Rogers, Mrs Olive Cowell, Mrs George Scherma of Rocky River Public Library, Dr Herbert Elwell, the reference librarian of Freiberger Library of Case-Western University, the librarians in the Music Division of Cleveland Public Library, Miss Dorothy Van Stripriaan; Dr Wayne Barlow, composer, of the Eastman School of Music, University of Rochester; William G Pottebaum, composer, and Lou Ouzer, photographer, of Rochester, New York; Robert Finn, Music Critic for the Cleveland Plain Dealer, and to those who so kindly read proof: my mother, the late Denise Koch, Dr John Diercks, Chairman of the Music Department of Hollins College in Virginia, and Mary Bill, General Manager of the Great Lakes Shakespeare Festival in Lakewood, Ohio.

HERBERT ELWELL

HERBERT ELWELL
1898-1974
a short biographical sketch

Though Cleveland was his home for many years, Herbert Elwell was born in Minneapolis, on May 10, 1898. It was there that he spent his boyhood and later studied piano and theory at the University of Minnesota. After World War I he studied composition with Ernest Bloch in New York and attended the newly established American Conservatory at Fontainebleau. In Paris he studied with Nadia Boulanger along with Aaron Copland, Virgil Thompson and Walter Piston.

I believe the Paris years were the happiest of his life, for his temperament was truly Parisian in that he fully enjoyed the pace of life, the cafe and the women. In 1923 he was awarded the three year Fellowship in Music at the American Academy in Rome. While there he conducted the first performance of his ballet suite *The Happy Hypocrite* with the Augusteo Orchestra.[1] It was in Paris that the *Quintet for Piano and Strings*[2] was performed by the composer on the same program with George Gershwin's *Rhapsody in Blue.* Of course at that time it was somewhat of a novelty for a serious work to employ jazz elements so that in the reviews all of the critical acclaim went to Herbert Elwell. He often chuckled over this. At this same time pianist Beveridge Webster performed a group of his piano pieces in Paris.

It was also in Paris that Elwell met his wife Maria, who is not French but Italian and, of all things, born in the United States in the state of Maine. After his marriage he returned to the United States where he accepted an offer to head the composition and advanced theory department of the Cleveland Institute of Music, a position he held for seventeen years. I remember meeting his wife Maria, who at that time spoke very little English, and it was difficult for her in social gatherings. However, she is truly a charming lady and one always enjoyed her company. Though her English much improved, she and her husband still spoke to one another in French.

It was during my undergraduate years at the Cleveland Institute of Music that I first met Herbert Elwell. I was a member of his harmony class and having just graduated from high school was somewhat in awe of him. I was soon inducted into military service so had to discontinue my music studies for about three years.

Upon my return in 1946 Elwell's *Lincoln Requiem* for baritone solo, chorus and orchestra won the Paderewski Prize and was presented by the Oberlin Choral Union in a nationwide broadcast. I remembered hearing this and being very much impressed with the work, as I had been with the performances of his many songs by the late Marie Simmelink Kraft.

In addition to his teaching, Herbert Elwell was music critic for the *Plain Dealer,* a position he held for thirty-two years. His Sunday column was a must on the reading list for all students, as were his reviews which were often controversial. I remember one time at a Cleveland Orchestra concert during which there was a terrible fit of coughing on the part of the audience. Szell stopped the orchestra and said that he would not continue until it was quiet; he left the podium. Everyone of course hacked away as loudly as he could and finally after a few minutes Szell strode onto the podium and fairly dove into the opening of the *Romeo and Juliet* Overture of Tchaikovsky. Elwell's headline the next day was 'Szell Puts Spur to Romeo' and in the course of the column remarked that it may be doubted whether anybody ever expected Romeo and Juliet to make love at a faster tempo. He also said, 'The orchestra was driven unmercifully at speeds which would certainly be frowned on by traffic officers, if not music critics.'

I was fortunate as a performing pianist to have had some favorable reviews by Herbert Elwell, though I must say all of us had heart palpitations when we knew he was out in the audience. He would come into the hall wearing a large borsalino hat and long overcoat, smoking a thin cigar. Without speaking a word to a soul he would walk to his seat and slump down in it; no one knew just what he might be like that night. One evening he attended a Cleveland Orchestra concert and slept through a good deal of the program. In the next morning's review he tore into the performance as though he had heard every note. I am sure he did in his subconscious mind for there was little that he missed.

The old Cox home was where the Cleveland Institute of Music held classes at East 36th and Euclid. It was a charming residence and had a most acoustically agreeable recital hall but a miserably small parking lot. This used to aggravate Elwell for invariably he would arrive late for the concert, having spent much time in search of a space to park. This never put him in a good frame of mind for listening.

As a composer he was most humble, but behind the typewriter Elwell sometimes took on monster proportions. He more than once got himself on the wrong side of fellow musicians for criticizing their antics, but for the most part he was fair and tried to pick out the good in the performance and if it wasn't good he just would not say a thing.

I remember one performance at the Cleveland Institute of Music in which Alice Chalifoux, harpist of the Cleveland Orchestra, was a participant. In this particular work Miss Chalifoux plucked several harmonic notes which struck Elwell funny and he had to leave the hall in a fit of laughter. Here was a very warm human being who enjoyed life to the full. All who knew him felt a warm bond of friendship, admired him as a musician and critic and overlooked his idiosyncrasies.

There was a memorable concert by John Cage at the Cleveland Museum of Art and Herbert Elwell came to review. Cage was performing a work with tape recorders and piano noises in which pianist David Tudor would knock on the wood underneath the piano, spin a gyroscope on the bass strings, or play random notes on the keyboard. At one point Tudor struck a delicious dominant ninth chord and Elwell rose to his feet and shouted 'BRAVO!' It practically broke up the place in gales of laughter, much to the consternation of loyal Cage devotees.

In 1961 Elwell was the first recipient of the Cleveland Arts Prize under the sponsorship of the Women's City Club. Herbert Elwell and his friend Robert E. Nelson, arranger, received acclaim in the summer of 1963 for writing a short (50 second) commercial for David Blauschild Chevrolet for which the Cleveland Orchestra was hired to play. It came in many versions — some with orchestra, with orchestra and voices, or with voices alone. *Newsweek*[3] carried a story and the headline was 'Don't Tell Szell.' It also made the front page of the *New York Times* and was aired via radio and over one hundred times per week for several months. Though Elwell said he would not do it again it proved to be a most successful venture.

I was grateful to have had a part, through the aegis of the West Shore Concerts that I founded, to present the Cleveland premiere of Elwell's *Concert Suite* for Violin and Orchestra.[4] Sidney Harth, for whom the work had been written, was soloist with the Cleveland Orchestra under the late George Szell. At that time Sidney and his wife Teresa, both former students of Elwell, were concertmaster and assistant of the orchestra.

The *Concert Suite* had been commissioned by the Louisville Orchestra. This orchestra came into prominence in 1948 when the Mayor made the suggestion to Robert Whitney, conductor, that a policy be initiated to commission a composer to write a work for world premiere on each subscription concert. By 1959 thirty-six LP twelve-inch recordings had been released and over one hundred thirty world premieres been given. This project played an important role in musical history in introducing new music to the general public and is still active today.

Whenever Sidney Harth played a solo, his wife moved up to the first chair. In order to show no partiality in this family affair, Herbert Elwell thoughtfully scored a short solo for the second concertmaster in the third movement. This was a thrilling performance of music that is dynamic, muscular and alive.

At this first hearing in Lakewood I remember that conductor Szell was a bit annoyed because the work had not been premiered first at Severance Hall and he did not attend the after-concert party and let Elwell take his bow with the orchestra alone. However, it was subsequently performed on the east side as a part of the May Festival of Music with Jerome Gross, violinist.

Upon leaving the Cleveland Institute of Music, Herbert Elwell continued teaching at the Oberlin Conservatory of Music and in the summer at the Eastman School of Music in Rochester. Upon completing my Masters degree, I renewed my contact with him as a private composition student and continued this study at the Eastman School. It was through his encouragement that I embarked on a doctoral program there. He has been a great influence on me and on such composers as Salvatore Martirano, John Diercks, Starling Cumberworth, Harold Miles, Walter Aschaffenberg, Bain Murray, Howard Whittaker and Werner Jepson.

Prior to his retirement from the *Plain Dealer* Elwell headed the composition department at the Cleveland Music School Settlement. Many of us had the pleasure of being with him on his 70th birthday at a party held in Howard Whittaker's home and we reminisced and heard many stories in his repertoire all rated X.

Many of the songs of Elwell have been sung by such well-known singers as James Melton, Donald Dame, Janet Fairbanks, Harold Haugh, Mildred Miller and Marie Simmelink Kraft.

Lately his good friend and arranger Robert E. Nelson did much to keep the name Elwell alive through numerous arrangements of his music for concert band.
Though at first Elwell didn't like the idea of his music being played by a band, I believe he was getting so many performances that he was very much impressed and pleased.

He retired from the *Plain Dealer* and his teaching. For many years he and his wife Maria led a quiet life in their Cleveland Heights home.

Herbert Elwell passed away Wednesday, April 17, 1974, in Cleveland.

[1] February 27, 1926
[2] April, 1928
[3] July 8, 1963
[4] March, 1959

HERBERT ELWELL
class notes on composing

Classes with Herbert Elwell were an inspiration for he was one of the most literate of musicians, in that he had a great appreciation for fine literature and poetry, and was very sensitive to words and their proper musical setting. He was also a most unassuming person who always was interested in whatever you had written and was always able to suggest ways to improve what you had done without changing drastically the style or original intent.

Many times considerable time was spent at the beginning of class in lighting a long thin cigarello. Should something displease him while looking at your music he would let go a burst of smoke so that it might take several minutes until the haze had cleared for you both to see the notes again.

He always stressed the logic of the bass line and had us work for strong outer voice parts. In song writing he suggested studying the poetry first for its 'arsic and thetic' tendencies and then to check the rhythm to see if it made musical sense.

In writing a song he felt it best not to deliberate in getting the voice started except when it is necessary to set the stage.

Moderato, tranquilo e semplice

from Agamede's Song (Arthur Upson) 1948

And at the end he felt it best to finish as soon as the voice is finished. This advice he follows in many of his own well wrought and most beautiful songs.

In the same song we find the voice finishing on a downbeat with its tied note over the bar while the piano finishes on the third beat of the following bar on low C.

sea - sons through

Herbert Elwell felt that a phrase should be set for that particular one and no other and that the song should contain a balance of short and long phrases. Unity can be achieved at the beginning and the end with even phrase lengths. Unevenness is a disintegrating factor and you don't want this early in the song unless the text suggests it. You find a perfect example of this in his song *The Road not Taken* with poem by Robert Frost in which the piano begins and ends with a four bar phrase.

We were always cautioned to study the line, the contour, the scale and to not always make the music suggest the feeling of the words as it spoils the poetic effect. It is important not to let musical ideas dictate.

The long singing line was stressed and we were urged to study some of the examples in the music of Faure and Berlioz. Such lines are ever evident in the Elwell song *All Foxes.*

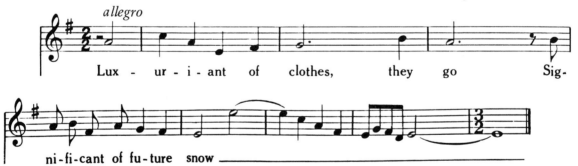

Lux - ur - i - ant   of   clothes,   they   go   Sig-

ni - fi - cant of fu - ture   snow

My notes contain the following directives: 'Don't be too timid in the presenting of your material, but be bold and hammer the idea home. Study the melody and make use of motives which prepare the listener for the unusual harmony by introducing it earlier. Above all be consistent in your harmonic procedure. Sometimes the principle motive or thematic idea can be the starting point for a voice. Two or three notes related intervallically or the motive varied in different rhythmic patterns might utilize the contrapuntal devices of canon or fugue. The finished product may be different from the one with which you started.' Elwell said that many times he would start out with an orchestral piece and end up with a song. He felt it important to always think of performance projection and how the idea will come off.

When counterpoint is introduced hang on to some of the 16th century practices as outlined by R.O. Morris in his book *16th Century Counterpoint,* and avoid regular accents always striving for good spacing of parts. When encountering a difficulty in working out an idea go back to what inspired the first sketch and try to recapture the original thought.

In some of the class discussion that we would have he said that some persons explain that it is easier to write music today since it is no longer necessary to observe any rules. To be sure the outer fringe of amateurs and dilettantes has enormously increased with the greater leisure and prosperity of the times. But it is hardly accurate to assume that all the rules have been thrown out of the window. He said, 'Coleridge was right in saying, 'Genius cannot be lawless; for it is even this that constitutes its genius — the power of acting creatively under laws of its own origination." or as Peter Vierick said in one of his poems, 'Art being the bartender, is never drunk.'

Many of the things that seem new, unorthodox and outrageous in the music of our time, have embryonic precedents and often real precedents in a past somewhat more remote than that covered by our scholastic experience. The minor third was once considered dissonant and chords like the diminished seventh and dominant ninth are now platitudinous. So what is to prevent one today from accepting chords of six, eight, ten, or even thirteen tones provided they make sense in their context? The sounds of nature, which we pretend to love, are infinitely more complex than the relationships of the first sixteen overtones of any given fundamental. In the best of our contemporary music the laws of melody and harmony have not been overthrown or negated, but rather expanded, or extended. It is true not only of melody and harmony, but also of rhythm.

Just as free verse has become common practice in poetry, irregular meter has become common practice in music. This does not mean that the laws of symmetry has become common practice in music. This does not mean that the laws of symmetry have been thrown to the winds. It means simply that music has recaptured some of the rhythmic subtlety and freedom it possessed before it fell into the fetters of pre-Victorian straight-jackets, the stolid parallel syntaxes of two plus two, four plus four, eight plus eight.

You find precedents for irregular meter in Gregorian chant, which of course has no bar lines. Were you to attempt to bar it, you would be forced into irregular alternation of duple and triple time. Rhythmic subtlety underlies the compositional structure of many an Elwell song. Primitive dances, Indian, African and other types give us abundant examples of irregular meter and much Oriental music breaks down into asymetrical complexity that Westerners have difficulty in following. In our own music, jazz was perhaps responsible for the beginning of greater rhythmic freedom. Not much music taught in the earlier grades today encourages a ready perception and execution of irregular meters and phrase groupings.

The form of a piece should grow out of the ideas and not be preconceived except when you are trying to fit ideas into a mold as in a clasic passacaglia, chaconne, etc. At all times ask yourself, are you being expressive?

Elwell felt that the music of Debussy and Stravinsky was well scored and that good orchestration can make something rather banal sound well. He warned against using extreme registers of trumpet, horn, trombone, and he thought that color through percussion is good if not done to excess. Remember all passages must move on — lead somewhere. In writing for orchestra, do not double parts unnecessarily for a clear score is preferred to one that is padded, and be sure to reinforce inner parts as well as the outer octaves. Consult orchestra players for bowings.

Consider development as growth similar to the parabola in variation form. One element should be constant as in this way it unifies like the sixteen measure phrase of the Beethoven *Diabelli Variations.* He didn't feel that variation form should be like the family album — just a series of unrelated pictures bearing no resemblance to the first. The irregularity of contrasting rhythm gives an urgency and unsettled feeling which at times can be good.

The more creative the artist, the more he develops intuition as his principal working tool. Because we all have a certain amount of intuition — in most cases, more intuition than knowledge — if a composer invites evaluation of his work solely on intuition, we feel entitled to criticize. Elwell pointed out that criticism is passing from the hands of the professional into the hands of the layman, the man who frankly admits he knows nothing about music, but jolly well knows what he likes. Well it is up to this man to find out a little more about why he likes *what* he likes, and to become a bit more *articulate* about it, because with all the intuitive powers in the world, the time has not yet come when an artist can create a masterpiece out of sheer ignorance, nor can his work be appreciated by a moron.

If on the other hand, this masterpiece is the result of superior intuition, it can be understood and enjoyed by anyone who has developed some degree of intuition, sympathy and love. For music, after all, is like love. It involves the coming together of kindred spirits in a domain which is agreeable and natural to them. The *great* music of our time will command this kind of affection. The *rest* does not matter.

Elwell said that his friend and teacher, Ernest Bloch, wrote much music that deserves to be called great. But he was never greater and perhaps one could say, never a better American, than when he expressed, with passion and devotion, musical elements that belonged specifically to his own race. 'He has never surpassed,' said Elwell, 'the works of his so-called Hebraic period, when he produced his magnificently eloquent rhapsody, *Schelomo,* his *Israel Symphony,* and the *Jewish Poems.* An element of compromise entered his work when, in his panoramic symphony, *America,* masterful as it was, he tried to 'write American!' It savored too much of the cheapness and sensationalism we associate with Hollywood, that lurid leveler of taste to a sickening common denominator.'

He commented further that when our composers learn to rely more upon their own first hand experiences, an American style *will* emerge, quite unconsciously, and we will recognize it by its quite extraordinary diversity of character.

To be sure, we have come a long way, and we are proud of it. But we also have a long way to go, and the destination will not be reached by walking blithely together, hand in hand, down a path strewn with fat commissions and flattering press notices. Some American composers today, far from being neglected, are almost pampered. Elwell said, 'I do not feel qualified to appraise the arts, but in our music there is too much sameness; and not enough independent leadership; and novelty, when it appears, is too often apt to be novelty for its own sake.'

Van Wyck Brooks said, 'The artist must stand alone, and listen to his intuitive whisperings.' Elwell said, 'Let us have our festivals, and work together, and compare notes when it interests us. Let us be socially collaborative, when situations call for it; but let us not become too complacent about our accomplishments, and let us remember to work in solitude and in honesty to ourselves, for only in this way can the artist best serve art and society.'

THREE POEMS OF ROBERT LIDDELL LOWE

You might say that everything Herbert Elwell wrote is a song for there is always a strong melodic line present and a great emotional quality which fully involves the listener. There is also a rich harmonic vocabulary, a great subtlety of rhythm and a strong bass line.

Herbert Elwell was very careful to select good poetry and you find such poets as Thomas Vautor, Arthur Upson, Robert Frost, D.H. Lawrence, and Pauline Hanson represented in his settings. His good friend Robert Liddell Lowe, who was Professor at Purdue University, wrote the texts for three poems, *All Foxes, This Glittering Grief,* and *Phoenix Afire* which are published by Fema Music Publishing Company of Chicago.

The first song *All Foxes* is a bright song and is one of my favorites. It should be mentioned that all of these songs were dedicated to the late Marie Simmelink Kraft, former Head of the Voice Department at the Cleveland Institute of Music; for it was she who introduced them at her annual voice recitals. Her projection seemed to be just right for the music and she became identified as the chief protagonist for Elwell's music.

The intervals of the third and sixth and also the tenth are a part of the musical texture of this song right in the beginning of the introduction. The use of melisma is used to advantage on the word 'sapience' and again at the end on the words 'approaching snow.'

The piano writing often engages in double or single octaves whichever seems most effective and a cumulative harmonic thrust is made by moving voices in contrary motion.

This occurs frequently and here just before the words 'small covenants.'

There is a subtle key change from *G* major with raised fourth step to *e* minor with the raised sixth step and a few measures later the use of the raised seventh step after which we return to the key of *G* and close with material taken from the introduction. A brilliant arpeggiated passage brings the song to conclusion on a *G* tonic. The use of rests in the accompaniment gives energy to the rhythm, and a rest is also often employed at the beginning of a phrase in the vocal line. Contrapuntal procedures are effectively used in the line 'with such supply' where the melody is in quarter notes and then on the next line with 'Men know which season is' the line is stated one-half step lower as an augmentation of the previous rhythm.

The idea of introducing something in the accompaniment before it is introduced in the voice is a device that Elwell stresses in his writing. See the accompaniment below before the words 'No mind's solitude' where the piano introduces the vocal line.

Great use is made of the inversion of intervals in both the vocal line and the piano part. The climax doesn't necessarily always come at the end for the voice line extends to a *G#* on the word 'beyond' which is the seventh of an *A#* half-diminished seventh chord and the high point of the song. The final *G* of the song on the word 'prophetic' is one-half step lower than the previous high point and it then drops one octave to one line *G* on the word 'weather' and the piano closes brilliantly with an arpeggiation on *G*.

These elements make an Elwell song a treat to study and re-study with always the same enjoyment and enthusiasm because this is vital, tonal, communicable music.

The second song *This Glittering Grief* makes use right at the beginning of an intriguing employment of the minor second.

The piano accompaniment has an *a* minor chord with a *B* flat coming in on the second beat. Interestingly enough this just announces something that happens at the end of the song on the words 'Tower tall' where there is a poly-chord of *C* major and *E* flat with an *F#* in the voice line creating that minor second which seems to depict the grief of the poetry.

In this same song we see the use of open fifths and fourths as a part of the modal harmonic scheme in both accompaniment and the vocal line.[5] The beginning of this song successfully avoids coming to any definite cadence for in the tenth measure you have a cadence on *D* but with the minor second in the upper voice of the piano part. Again in measure 19 you have a cadence on *F* with a seventh in the bass giving it a feeling of indefiniteness. The presence of the *E* flat gives the suggestion of Phrygian mode.

The second page becomes more definite harmonically and makes use of a wonderful descending bass starting with the *D* flat in measure 32 and progressing downward C, B, A flat, G, F, E flat, D natural, D flat. The enharmonic spelling is used as the *D* flat ascends to *F#* or G flat (3rd or 4th relation) and in the piano right hand we find the use of the minor third and minor sixth.

Herbert Elwell was most careful to have the vocal part end on words which sing well. In the English language one does have a problem because of the many explosive consonants.

We see here the successful use of modified sequential repetition on the words 'wrote transiently.'

The three statements 'of grieving' are each set in the voice in different rhythms and these words always enter after a rest which enhances the word painting.

The piano interlude following introduces some of the quality of the beginning in the evasion of definite cadential feeling, but it again returns to functional progression in the part leading up to a climax on the words 'Tower tall.' This superimposed harmony sounds like an eleventh chord on *C* with an *E* flat and the song closes on the words 'too lovely for oblivion.' Evoking the mood of the poetry the harmony comes to rest on a Phrygian cadence leaving the listener in somewhat of a suspenseful atmosphere.

The final song *Phoenix Afire* demands bravura technique on the part of the pianist. Herbert Elwell was a really fine pianist as any one can testify who heard him play for Marie Simmelink Kraft which he did on rare occasions in Cleveland, Oberlin and Rochester. He had considerable facility and a marvelous sense for the musical interpretation.

The song shifts between the keys of *A* major with raised fourth step and *C* major with lowered seventh step and begins with this spreading of the major-minor sonorities building in a pyramidal stack of thirds until the voice enters. In the middle of the piano part marked *leggiero* a tricky triplet accompaniment figure is introduced in the right hand against a syncopated part for the left. The rhythmic interest is definitely in the piano with the voice often holding notes.

This section ends with the voice on the word 'way' holding a *C* as the piano continues its triplet figuration ending on the dominant *G* as the seventh of a major-minor ninth on *F* over an *E* flat chord.

The fourth page is rich harmonically with the use of planing modal harmonies. Here we see more of the Elwellian double octave piano style and harmonies comprised of thirds and sixths as well as open fifths. Intensity is built up by the repetition of the phrase 'consumes itself in proper flame.' The climax on the high *A* on the word 'rise' anticipates the closing of the next page.

After a long building passage of fifths we head toward a fortissimo again on the high *A* and the piano then resumes its tricky passage work for eight bars to end the song with excitement.

The songs of Herbert Elwell are rewarding to work on but require good musicianship on the part of both singer and pianist to perform them successfully. They contain a beautiful vocal line which does much to complement the voice as Metropolitan Opera singer Mildred Miller will tell you for she sings many of these songs on her numerous concert tours.

There is an involvement in an Elwell song unlike any others that you might hear that should make them remain a part of the vocal repertoire for many years to come.

[5] *This Glittering Grief,* p.8

THE MUSIC OF HERBERT ELWELL

Date	ORCHESTRA	*Publisher*
1925	*The Happy Hypocrite* music for the ballet based on the story by Max Beerbohm	Carl Fischer Inc.
1942	Introduction and Allegro	
1948	*Pastorale* for voice and orchestra based on passages from *The Song of Solomon*	Fema Music (rental)
1950	*Ode for Orchestra*	Boosey & Hawkes (rental)
1953	*The Forever Young* for voice and orchestra based on a text by Pauline Hanson	Fema Music (rental)
1957	*Concert Suite* for violin and orchestra	Rochester Music Publishers
1966	*Symphonic Sketches* Commissioned for the 50th anniversary of the Cleveland Museum of Art	
	CHORUS	
1937	Cantata: *I was with Him* Tenor solo, male choir (two pianos)	
1944	Five Songs for Men's Voices (After Li-Po)	
1947	*Lincoln Requiem Aeternam* — mixed chorus, baritone solo and orchestra, based on a text by John Gould Fletcher	

PIANO

1926	Sonata	Oxford
1928	Pieces for piano: Prelude, Cortege, Berceuse, Dance	Rochester Music Publishers
1930	Three Preludes	Rochester Music Publishers
1947	For young pianists: Bus Ride, Tarantella, Plaint, Procession	Carl Fischer Inc. T. Presser

SONGS

1940	Agamedes Song (Arthur Upson)	Valley Music Press
1950	Christmas Carol (Marian Berry Simpson)	G. Schirmer
	In the Mountains (Chang Yu)	
	Music I Heard with You (Conrad Aiken)	G. Schirmer
	Renouncement (Alice Meynell)	G. Schirmer
	The Road not Taken (Robert Frost)	G. Schirmer
	Suffolk Owl (Thomas Vautor)	Valley Music Press
	All Foxes, This Glittering Grief, Phoenix Afire (Robert Liddell Lowe)	Fema Music Inc.
	The Waters of Pain (Tudor Hart)	
	Le pays des enfants Joyeux (Tudor Hart)	
	The Palantine (Cather)	
	He whom a dream hath possessed (O'Sheel)	
	Love Charm of Simaitha (Theocritus-Robinson)	
	I Look Back (Pauline Hanson)	
	A Child's Grace (Carlin)	
	Song Against Songs (Chesterton)	
	The Ouselcock (Shakespeare)	
	Tarantella, Giorno dei morti, In a Boat (D.H. Lawrence)	Fema Music Inc.
	Wistful (from the Chinese)	Lawson Gould
	American Psalm (David Morton)	

*The G. Schirmer and Valley Music Press publications are out of print but available at the Cleveland Public Library or Sibley Library of the Eastman School of Music.

CHAMBER MUSIC

| 1923 | Quintet for Piano and Strings |
| 1927 | Sonata for Violin and Piano |

1926	Divertimento for String Quartet	
1937	String Quartet No. 1 in e minor	
1945	*Blue Symphony* for voice and string quartet	Rochester Music Publishers
1953	Variations for Violin and Piano	Rochester Music Publishers

CONCERT BAND — Arrangements by Robert E. Nelson

1960	Dance of the Merry Dwarfs	Ludwig Music Co.
	Poeme	Concert Music (Bourne Music Inc.)
1961	Overture	Carl Fischer
1962	Procession	C.L. Barnhouse
1964	Evocation, Rhapsody (rental)	Fema Music Inc.
1967	Exhortation	Fema Music Inc.
1969	Scherzo	Concert Music (Bourne Music Inc.)
1974	Gregorian Overture	Ludwig Music Co.
1974	Reminiscence	

ARTICLES BY AND ABOUT HERBERT ELWELL

'Is Theory for Composers Only?' *Musician,* November, 1928, p. 33.

'Copland, America's Young Man of Promise,' *Modern Music,* April, 1926, p. 14-15.

'Ballet — The Happy Hypocrite,' criticism, Cleveland Orchestra program, 12th season, p. 575-577.

ARTHUR SHEPHERD

George Hauenstein

ARTHUR SHEPHERD
1880-1958
a short biographical sketch

Paris, Idaho, a little settlement in the colorful Bear Lake Valley, was the city in which
Arthur Shepherd was born on February 19, 1880. His parents, who were English, emigrated
to America in 1877 and were converts to Mormonism. His early recollections were of the
family reed organ. He began music lessons at an early age and showed marked ability. His
father displayed admirable intelligence and sympathy for he packed young Arthur off at age
twelve to The New England Conservatory in Boston. It was either Boston or Leipzig and
Boston won out.. His two brothers, Charles and Albert, also chose to enter the field of
music. Arthur's teachers were Benjamin Cutter and Dr. Percy Goetschius, both of whom
were trained in Germany. The result was Shepherd's obvious thoroughness and his mastery
of part-writing. Denoe Leedy in an article in *Modern Music* said, 'Percy Goetschius, a veritable gibraltar of theoretical stability, dispensed sound instruction and inspired the eager
Idaho musician to write.'[1]

Arthur was a facile sight reader and was much in demand as an accompanist. He graduated in pianoforte with honors and was the President of his class. Following graduation he
located in Salt Lake City where his family then lived and for twelve years he devoted himself to teaching privately, composing, and organizing and conducting concerts. In 1902 his
Overture Joyeuse won the Paderewski Prize and was performed in New York by a Russian
Orchestra and in Salt Lake by the New York Symphony under Walter Damrosch.

Arthur Shepherd was interested for several years in a publishing enterprise known as
Wa-Wan Press sponsored by Arthur Farwell and this brought him to Boston in 1909. In
1910 he decided to locate there permanently and became a faculty member of his alma
mater, the New England Conservatory of Music, in the department of harmony. He conducted the Cecilia Society and had several large works performed with the assistance of
members of the Boston Symphony Orchestra.

It was through the Wa-Wan Press, and the movement that centered around it, that
Arthur Farwell made his most significant contribution to the advancement of America's
music. It brought out a song collection and several piano pieces by Shepherd.

In the preliminary announcement, Farwell stated: 'The Wa-Wan Press is a natural out-
come of the rapid growth of true musical genius in America, and in proportion to its capacity and growth, will aim to render available hitherto unpublished compositions of the high-
est order, which because of circumstances which the art-life of America is rapidly outgrow-
ing, have heretofore been denied the daylight of print.' The enterprise was launched without
capital and without financial backing of any kind. Farwell engaged a printer in Newton
Center, Massachusetts, borrowed a few dollars for postage, and set out to get subscribers.
The music engraving and lithography were done in Boston. The plan was to bring out two
books of music each quarter; later the publications were also issued separately, in sheet-
music form. The enterprise continued for eleven years and the catalogue was then turned
over to the firm of G. Schirmer.[2]

Arthur Shepherd served overseas during World War I and was the band master of 303rd
Massachusetts Field Artillery Band. His greatest thrill came at Creue, France when he played
for villagers on the morning of the Armistice.

In 1920 he was chosen by Nikolai Sokoloff to be Assistant Conductor of the newly
formed Cleveland Orchestra. He remained in Cleveland thereafter for the rest of his life. For

seven years he was the conductor of the Pops concerts, the Children's concerts, served as Music Critic for the *Cleveland Press,* edited the Cleveland Orchestra program notes, and was always on call for performances, lectures and arrangements of musical events.

Arthur Shepherd said that one of his most satisfactory experiences was when he was conducting the Cleveland Orchestra in the first performance of the 9th Symphony of Beethoven. During the time that he was assistant conductor, Adella Prentiss Hughes, one of the founders of the orchestra, introduced him to his future wife, Grazella Puliver. Mrs. Shepherd admits that she was very impressed at this first meeting and went home and told her mother that this man was the finest man she had ever met. It wasn't long after that they were married. Their son, Peter, today is in the publishing business in New York. By a previous marriage Arthur Shepherd had two sons, Arthur and Richard, and a daughter, Mrs. George Odell.

He served as Professor of the Western Reserve Music Department of which he was Head from 1933-1948. The University conferred an honorary doctorate upon him in 1937 and that same year he was elected to membership in the National Institute of Arts and Letters.

It was during my student days at the Cleveland Insitute of Music that I first heard Arthur Shepherd give a lecture for the fine arts series. I was most impressed by his great knowledge and by the strength and conviction of his music. Upon graduation from the Institute I enrolled at Western Reserve University to work toward a Masters degree and there was a member of his counterpoint class. Here I came in close contact with a man who loved counterpoint and made it a fascinating study. He would work painstakingly over our exercises to get the right voice leading and interval relationships. I also participated in his composition class and began to take an interest in modal harmony. He encouraged me in the writing of some children's pieces which were later published, and the Sonatina (1950) for piano that I wrote under his tutelage won the Homer B. Hatch Award in Composition from the Fortnightly Music Club.

Later as Director of the West Shore Concerts, a concert course that I founded, I presented a performance of his *Overture to a Drama* with the Cleveland Philharmonic Orchestra under F. Karl Grossman in February, 1954.

Some friends and I presented a contemporary music concert in February, 1955 in Willard Clapp Hall of the Cleveland Institute of Music and pianist Arthur Loesser performed Shepherd's Second Piano Sonata. Upon his retirement I continued to visit his private studio and show him my work from time to time and he was always interested and helpful. One of his last works was a *Theme and Variations on an Original Theme* which was performed by the Cleveland Orchestra in 1955 under the late George Szell. His last String Quartet no. 4 was commissioned by the Chamber Music Society of Cleveland and was presented by the Kroll String Quartet.

Many of his students such as composer Alvin Etler and William S. Newman, musicologist, have received national acclaim. Former student and New York pianist, Vivian Harvey Slater, has been a champion of his piano music as has Cleveland pianist, the late Arthur Loesser.

He once said, 'Hard work, my family, the life of a student were the chief joys of my life.' He enjoyed giving his son a dubbing at tennis, and delving into old books for reading was his hobby. Arthur Shepherd died in Cleveland on January 12, 1958.

His whole life was a series of conscious choices and he chose to enhance beauty rather than bow to despair or defeat — both of which he knew well. He often said, 'One must choose.' The poems which he set to music reveal a revered love of nature which was sustained throughout his life. He was attracted to the lyrical and the spiritual. To those who knew him well his wit and humor were a delight and these are reflected in several of his compositions.

Colleague F. Karl Grossman said of Shepherd's music, 'His music seems to have a certain quality (some think like what Wyndam Lewis had to say regarding the poetry of Francois Villon) that will make it wear; it seems like the man himself, you like it better the more you get to know it.'

Cleveland pianist-harpsichordist Frieda Schumacher did much to preserve the name of Arthur Shepherd by inaugurating an Arthur Shepherd Composition Contest. It continued during her chairmanship under the auspices of the Ohio Music Teachers Association for ten years.

In an article in the *Musical Quarterly* it was said of Arthur Shepherd, 'Characteristic of his whole outlook is the way that he grows out of, not revolts against tradition. Though he is hardly among the vanguard of the 'modernists' he pays remarkably close attention to their activities. In his teaching and in his own work he showed the characteristic intent of his contemporaries in a return to counterpoint, or what he has described as a 'third incarnation of the polyphonic style.'[3]

His best known work is the orchestral piece *Horizons* published in a Juillian Edition. It was performed by the Cleveland Orchestra under Leopold Stokowski and it was also heard in Paris, Warsaw and Prague. The movement entitled 'The Old Chisholm Trail' was recorded by the Cleveland Pops Orchestra under Louis Lane.

The work consists of four Western pieces: Westward, the Lone Prairie (based on an old Cowboy song of the late Henry F. Gilbert), The Old Chisholm Trail in which he employs the tenor saxophone, and Canyons — Hymn of Western Pioneers. A big orchestra was employed with four percussion, four horns, four trumpets in C, one trumpet in D, trombone, tuba and tenor saxophone in addition to strings and winds. The flair of the folk song pervades the entire score.

The Arthur Shepherd files were in the archives of Freiberger Library of Case-Western Reserve University and are now in the library of the University of Utah at Salt Lake City, Utah. They contain letters from Howard Hanson, Edward Burlingame Hill, Arthur Farwell, Leopold Stokowski, Artur Rodzinski, George Szell and others. The scope of these letters makes you realize that Arthur Shepherd played a vital role in the history of American music.

ARTHUR SHEPHERD
class notes on composing

Studying with Arthur Shepherd made one appreciate the complete sincerity of a painstaking craftsman who was most critical of his own as well as his students' work. He might be described as a serious professorial type but there was always a twinkle in his eye for he had a keen sense of humor. In an article in *Modern Music* Denoe Leedy said of him, 'Distinguished in bearing to the public and friendly, scholarly — he writes too many notes.'[3]

His music was subject to his own critical scrutiny of a devastating and merciless nature for he changed, corrected, revised and rewrote without regard to practical considerations of performance or publication. One of the statements which he made in class that I found most helpful was not to analyze your work until you have to but then know how to do it. He felt that clarity, simplicity and rationality were key watch words. Much of this stemmed from his early background as a student of Percy Goetschius. He often referred to the book *Homophonic Forms* by his former teacher.

He felt that the success of a work depended upon 'good structure and good sound,' and given that — an inspiration had a chance to be heard. In analyzing one's music he rarely changed the idea inherent in the music but helped improve it.

As young fledglings he encouraged us to understand the normal tendencies in music and form and then deviate if we must and be willing to take the consequences. Like Herbert Elwell he encouraged us to keep in mind at all times the melodic contour and what the melody implied harmonically. We were also to consider carefully the style and setting of each piece. He felt it important to know how to get from the *A* theme to the *B* in a convincing manner and to have control of the thematic idea. 'Let it develop logically,' he would say. Often we were reminded that if we struck upon something expressive, to remember it and use it again. He followed his own advice in many of his own compositions.

Arthur Shepherd set high standards for quality and urged us to consult good models in the works of Brahms, Faure, Debussy, Ravel and Hindemith. He often quoted Ruskin who said, 'In Art one thing must prevail,' in music — melody, rhythm and harmony. Rhythm as well as notes can give expressiveness. He would say that looking backward after you have made a new start gives unity by using old material over. He saw to it that we studied the harmonies of the style in which we wrote so that there might be logic. He preferred that we not write things momentarily disturbing but to strive for consistency in the use of dissonance.

We were to take a workman-like approach to our work as we decided upon rhythm, design, key and meter. He would often say, 'The bass is important — give especial attention to it.'

We were to avoid banality in the cadences — and to think of chord progression and not chord resolution. He felt the gestalt theory workable in composition — the whole, then the parts. The re-harmonization of melodic fragments — giving a new setting was considered good. How to repeat and keep ideas fresh and interesting is the composer's problem and this he would say keeps us working.

He utilized a sketchbook method for his own composition and in looking at these sketches you realize what a metamorphosis an idea of his went through. His *Theme and Variations* for Orchestra was first conceived as a piano work written on three staves. He even made a key distribution analysis and the whole work was laid out as carefully as though in final form.

These quotations of his are memorable: 'Away with esoteric ears — leave them to the donkey,' and 'If innocence of the eye is a characteristic attribute of the great painter, innocence of the ear may account for the most precious moments in music.' He never forgot exercises and was always working counterpoint problems like others might work the crossword puzzles.

The melody used for a variation form must be good and the composer should be critical in selecting the model. In writing we were not allowed to go too far afield from ground we were sure of and we were urged to use the contrapuntal method of study. He would always say that the ear is the final court of appeal to reject or approve.

In writing for piano a thin style was preferred sometimes utilizing just three parts. And we were to make it all flow. It was pointed out that in three part writing we were dealing with an incomplete chord and thus the sonority was not a problem but the doubling freer. 'Consult the *Two and Three Part Inventions* of J.S. Bach and read the chapter on 'Three Part Writing' in the *Oxford Book of Harmony* by R.O. Morris.' These and other directions were in my notes.

Examples of three part writing in his own works can be seen in his well wrought *Second Sonata for Piano* in the second movement. The *Toccata* in the last movement combines alternating rhythms of 3/8 and 4/8 and is a tour de force for the pianist. This sonata was a favorite of the late Arthur Loesser of Cleveland who performed it brilliantly.

Variety in unity — phrase form — balance is necessary. He once said, 'I myself consider the totality of a piece the idea.'

He felt the inner rhythm, the turn of phrase and the spirit were the requisites for a song and that the words themselves should be musical. He set to music forty odd poems among which there is a preponderance of English and Irish poetry. He chose poems that were descriptive or fanciful and liked those that had a folk song quality. He always respected the poet's intentions and let it determine the form of the musical setting. *Where Loveliness Keeps House* with poetry of Madison Cawein is typical of his closeness to nature and has a philosophy of peacefulness and harmony about it. *The Fiddlers* with words of Walter de la Mare has a touch of humor. He encouraged us to study the vowel sounds and quoted from his song *Virgil* with poetry of Oliver St. John Gogarty.

'From Mantua's meadows to Imperial Rome
came Virgil with the woodlight in his eyes.'

'Listen to the m's in the first line,' he would say. His own search for inspiration led him to the poem of a child as well as to those of the great poets and philosophers.

In the setting of words he relied on rhythm, accentuation, and meaning of the text, to determine the rhythm of the melody, phrase lengths, high and low tones, and climaxes.

A recording was made of sixteen of his beautiful songs sung by the late Marie Simmelink Kraft, mezzo-soprano, with Marianne Mastics, pianist, and was produced by Case-Western Reserve University. Herbert Elwell wrote, 'These songs offer a more complete picture of Shepherd, the man and the musician than anything we have yet heard. They are his philosophic reaction to life.'

Arthur Shepherd said that the artist today must have a broader horizon than ever before so widespread have become his materials. His personal creed and advice to young composers is the following: 'To be himself, to express himself, to trust God and his fellow man, to look into his heart and write.'

TRIPTYCH FOR HIGH VOICE AND STRING QUARTET

Arthur Shepherd's conspicuous success is as a melodist. He is at his best when he hits upon a good tune. Most often his melodies are folkish and modal in character. His favorite modal inflections appear to be the lowered second and the raised fourth degree.

His setting of the poetry of Tagore is among the best which has come from his pen. He has written with spontaneity and lyrical fervor and a highly perceptive treatment of the text. The *Triptych* was published by the Society for the Publication of American Music and recorded by the Walden String Quartet with Marie Simmelink Kraft, mezzo-soprano. There are three sections, the first: 'He it is,' the second: 'The day is no more,' and the third: 'Light, my light.' It was dedicated to Adella Prentiss Hughes who had so much to do with the founding of the Cleveland Orchestra.

There is a tonic-sub-dominant key relationship in the first section which goes from *E* flat to *A* flat and then back again. This expressive motive is used again throughout the first movement.

You see the use of the lowered seventh step, a characteristic feature of Shepherd's work and the importance of the interval of the fifth and its inversion, the fourth. The opening melody of the voice has a beautiful contour and slips downward by minor third and then major third.

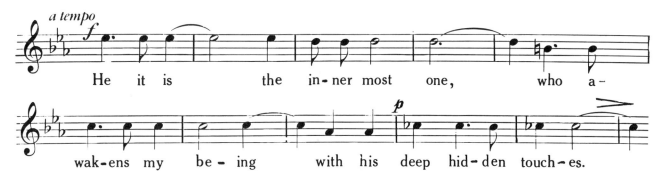

We see the third relationship in key structure on page three of the score as the movement moves momentarily from *E* flat Mixolydian mode to *G* and then back. We then go from *E* flat to *A* major, a raised subdominant, which is a surprise. There is an effective use of the sequence in the vocal lines with the words 'Of gold and silver — blue and green.' On page seven there is adept orchestration of the words 'at whose touch' in which the strings first hold a *g* minor chord pianissimo and then on the word 'touch' a *G* major-minor seventh with an added sixth. The first violin takes the root of the chord as a harmonic.

The viola has this very lyric solo on page six of the score.

The strings have some very beautiful writing in the section marked 'Divuto e sonora-mente.' The climax in this section comes on the word 'rapture' with the voice taking a high *B* flat and the second violin and viola engaging in triplet passage work. The voice uses an effective glissando device on the word 'sorrow' on page nine,

and the section closes with the little motive with which it began only this time it is stated in the cello. The section is tripartite in form and the use of contrapuntal harmony prevails as it does in much of Arthur Shepherd's work.

The second movement 'The day is no more' is basically in *e* minor and the presence of a raised 6th step in the vocal line suggests transposed Dorian mode. The minor third is the strong interval in this movement. The strings begin on a pizzicato *B* the dominant note, and the voice begins quietly in a semi-parlando style. The interval G-D# opens and closes this movement. It is first introduced in the second violin and then it is again sounded at the close in this same part.

At the bottom of page eleven in the score we see in the strings a section in 2/2 in which there is a great deal of rhythmic independence of parts. At the 'poco piu animato' the key changes to *B* major with the raised fourth step suggesting Lydian mode. There is an effective use of pedal point in the cello.

Scholarly Shepherd uses the tempo mark 'poco ravivamente' (a little quickening) for the closing section. The final ten bars marked 'ben parlando' are colorful harmonically with the first violin employing harmonics. The harmony at this place begins with a *b* minor chord then goes to a *G* seventh with a superimposed dissonance of an *F#* chord and then back to a *G* triad and finally ending with a *G* augmented chord. The strings close on a *B* as they began. This movement is very atmospheric and forward looking for the twenties when it was written.

The third section 'Light, my light' is in *e* minor (transposed Dorian) and combines 9/8 and 6/8 into a scherzo-like finale. The use of tremolando in the strings gives an urgency to the beginning.

The strings in the introduction build up to a tremolando on a *C#* diminished seventh chord to the opening words of the voice. It begins solidly on a *G* major chord so if you consider the root of the *C#* diminished seventh to be *A* you then have a II-I harmonic relationship.

Syncopation of the vocal line is employed and at section (A) the scherzando section begins.

eye-kiss-ing   heart sweet-'ning   light! _____

Ah, the light danc-es, my dar-ling,   at the cen-tre of my life;

This section (A) is in *G* with lowered seventh (Mixolydian mode) and then there is a transition to *E* flat (transposed Lydian). The voice part reaches a climax on high *G* flat on the words 'my darling.' There are effective sequential phrase repetitions on the phrase 'the flood of joy' with a high *G* in the vocal line after which the strings again elaborate on this C# diminished chord that had led up to the word 'light' at the beginning. This time it is done more intensely until in unison all four strings fortissimo move upward (E-F#-G), and after a fermata, the voice comes in again with the words 'Light, my light.'

The whole tone scale may be seen in the first violin part under the final words 'world filling light' as the notes descend (G, F E flat, C flat) and then brilliant passage work in the quartet brings the work to a close on a *G* major chord.

You are aware throughout of the superb craftsmanship of the composer, the skillful handling of the string parts, and of the compelling vocal line. This is an exciting work with many moments of melodic tenderness.

THE MUSIC OF ARTHUR SHEPHERD

Date	ORCHESTRAL WORKS	Publisher
1901	Overture Joyeuse	Manuscript
1915	Overture, The Festival of Youth	Manuscript
1916	Fantasy for Piano and Orchestra	Manuscript
1919	Overture to a Drama	C.C. Birchard
1927	Horizons, Symphony No. 1	C.C. Birchard
1931	Choreographic Suite	Manuscript

1938	Symphony No. 2 in D	Manuscript
	Fantasia Concertante	Manuscript
1946	Fantasia on 'Down East Spirituals'	Manuscript
1946-7	Concerto for Violin and Orchestra	Manuscript
1955	Theme and Variations for Orchestra on an original theme	Manuscript

CONCERT BAND

| 1944 | Overture Hilaritas | Carl Fischer |

CHORAL WORKS

1908	The Lord hath brought again Zion (motet mixed voices, baritone solo)	Oliver Ditson
1913	The City in the Sea (Cantata with orchestra)	Boston Music
1915	Song of the Sea Wind (Women's voices)	A.P. Schmidt Co.
	He came all so still (Women's voices)	A.P. Schmidt Co.
1918	O Jesu Who are gone before (Anthem)	Boston Music
	Deck thyself my soul (Response, mixed voices, organ)	Boston Music
1935	Ballad of Trees and the Master (mixed a cappella)	C.C. Birchard
1937	Invitation to the Dance (Text by Sidonius Appolinaris)	Manuscript
1938	Build thee more stately mansions (Women's voices)	Manuscript
	Grace for Gardens (Mixed, a cappella)	Arrow Press
	Planting a Tree (Mixed voices)	Manuscript
	Slowly Silently Now the Moon (Women's voices)	Manuscript
	Psalm XLII (chorus/orchestra)	Manuscript
	Carol	Music Press
	Jolly Wat	Music Press
	Drive on (mixed chorus)	Manuscript
1958	Psalm of the Mountains (Text by Judge Florence Allen)	Manuscript

CHAMBER MUSIC

1926	Triptych for High Voice and String Quartet	S.P.A.M.-T. Presser
1927	Sonata for Violin and Piano	Edition Maurice Senart
1928	Quartet for Strings No. 1 g minor	Manuscript
1935	Quartet for Strings No. 2 e minor	S.P.A.M.-J. Fisher
1936	Quartet for Strings No. 3 g minor	Manuscript
1940	Quintet for Piano and Strings	J. Fischer & Son
1942	Praeludium for Wind Instruments and Strings	Manuscript
1955	Quartet for Strings No. 4	Manuscript

PIANO WORKS

1903	Theme and Variation	Wa-Wan Press
1905	Mazurka — Prelude	Wa-Wan Press
	Sonata No. 1 f minor	Boston Music
1912	Prelude and Fugue in e minor	Manuscript
	Fugue in C sharp minor	Manuscript
1929	From a Mountain Lake	Manuscript
1930	Exotic Dance	Oxford Univ. Press
	Sonata No. 2 f minor	Oxford Univ. Press
1931	Gigue Fantasque	Manuscript
	Eclogue	T. Presser
1932	Two Preludes	Carl Fischer
1936	Autumn Fields	Carl Fischer
	Gay Promenade	Carl Fischer
1938	Lento Amabile	T. Presser
	Capriccio	Manuscript
	Song	Manuscript
1939	Two-Step	Manuscript
1941	Exotic Dance No. II and III	Manuscript
	Capriccio No. II	G. Ricordi

	Nocturne	Manuscript
	Capriccio No. III	Manuscript
	Scherzino	Manuscript
	Souvenir	Manuscript
	Whimsy in G	Manuscript
	In Mode Ostinato	T. Presser

SONGS

1909	Five songs, on Poems of James Russell Lowell	Wa-Wan Press
	The Gentle Lady (John Masefield)	
	Oh like a Queen	
	Where Loveliness keeps house (Madison Cawein)	
	Softly along the road of evening (Walter de la Mare)	
1948	The Fiddlers (Walter de la Mare)	Valley Music Press
	Reverie (Walter de la Mare)	Valley Music Press
	Bacchus (Frank Dempster Sherman)	
	Golden Stockings (Oliver St. John Gogarty)	
	Virgil (Oliver St. John Gogarty)	
	To a Trout (Oliver St. John Gogarty)	
	The Charm (Campion)	
	April (Sarah Teasdale)	
	Matin Song (Thoms Heywood)	
	Heart's Journey (Siegfried Sassoon)	
	Morning Glory (Siegfried Sassoon)	
	Serenade (Edith Sitwell)	
	The Starling Lake (Seumas O'Sullivan)	Valley Music Press
	The Chambered Nautilus (Oliver Wendell Holmes)	
	In the Scented Bud of the Morning (James Stephens)	
	The Lost Child (James Russell Lowell)	
	Sunday up the River (James Thomson)	

ORGAN

Fantasia on the 'Garden Hymn'   H.W. Gray

BOOKS AND ARTICLES ON MUSIC *

1925   Listening in on the Masters
        Alice Keith in collaboration with Arthur
        Shepherd, Director of Young People's
        Concerts of the Cleveland Orchestra   C.C. Birchard

1935   *The String Quartets of Ludwig von Beethoven*
        Historic and analytic commentaries by Arthur
            Shepherd. Cleveland, Horace Carr, the
            Printing Press.

        Several articles in *Cobbett's Cyclpedic
            Survey of Chamber Music.*

        Papa Goetschius in Retrospect, Musical
            Quarterly XXX No. 3, July, 1944, pp.
            307-318.

        *unless publisher is shown the work is in manuscript.

ARTICLES BY AND ABOUT ARTHUR SHEPHERD

Music in America, p. 417-419 — The Art of Music, vol. 4

Groves Dictionary of Music and Musicians, American Supplement, p. 381.

American Composers — Hughes — p. 504-506.

International Who's Who in Music — p. 588.

The New Encyclopedic of Music and Musicians, Pratt, p. 755.

Musiklexikon, Riemann vol. 2 p. 1698-99.

Cleveland Orchestra Programs (1929-30)
    Vol. II 257-263 (Notes on Horizons by Arthur Loesser).

BERNARD ROGERS

G. Mauersberger

BERNARD ROGERS
1893-1968
a short biographical sketch

Bernard Rogers was born on February 4, 1893 in Yorksville, New York. His father, Solomon Rogers, was a jeweler. Young Bernard attended the public schools of New York City and New Rochelle. His first creative efforts were at painting when he was twelve and he pursued this art with great zeal without sustained instruction of any kind. He was given piano lessons but took no interest in this instrument. A few years later he heard his first orchestra concert, a Young People's Symphony conducted by Frank Damrosch. It was a revelation and he knew then that music was to be his craft and that he was to dedicate his life to it.

His first teachers in theory and composition were Arthur van den Berg and Arthur Farwell. In 1916 he became the first American student of Ernest Bloch who was teaching in New York City. He studied architecture briefly at Columbia University while working evenings at the firm of Carrere and Hastings. He enrolled at the Institute of Musical Art (now Juilliard School of Music) in 1920 where he studied theory with Percy Goetschius and later went to Cleveland to continue his work with Bloch who had been appointed Director of the Institute of Music. While in Cleveland Rogers served as music critic for the Cleveland Commercial.

After the success of his symphonic elegy *To the Fallen* introduced by Josef Stransky and the New York Philharmonic in 1919, Rogers was awarded a Pulitzer Traveling Scholarship for study in Europe.

He joined the staff of Musical America in 1913 and remained on the editorial staff and as critic off and on until 1924. He had left home to live independently and his work at Musical America was his sole means of support in these early years.

He married his first wife Lillian Soskin in 1916 and was divorced in 1933 and then in 1934 he married a student, Anne Day Thacher who died in 1935. He has one daughter Anne Rogers Zehnder and three grandchildren. His present widow Elizabeth Clark, was also a former student and is a lovely lady. According to his friend Herbert Elwell, she is also a good composer and copyist.

Rogers was a faculty member of the Julius Hartt School of Music in Connecticut for the year 1926-27 and in 1927 he received a Guggenheim Fellowship at which time he did further work with Nadia Boulanger in Paris and Frank Bridge in London. Accompanied by his first wife Lillian, and his associate at Musical America, Charles Rodda, he settled in Kent and later in Paris. While in Paris he composed his first choral music 'The Raising of Lazarus' with text by his wife.

It was during the years that Bernard Rogers worked for Musical America that he met Dr. Howard Hanson who at that time was the Director of the Eastman School of Music. Hanson invited him to Rochester to teach composition and orchestration at the school. Rogers joined the faculty in 1929 and in the ensuing thirty-eight years taught more than 700 composers many of whom have achieved international prominence.

The Ford Foundation, Koussevitzky Foundation, the Louisville Orchestra and several other organizations commissioned works by him, and he has received many awards such as the David Bispham Medal for Opera in 1947; and the Lillian Fairchild Award in 1962 to name a few.

His manual 'The Art of Orchestration' has been acknowledged a classic in its field since its publication in 1951. Bernard Rogers held honorary doctorates from Valparaiso University and Wayne State University and became a member of the National Institute of Arts and Letters in 1947.

I was introduced to Bernard Rogers through Herbert Elwell while working on a doctoral program at the Eastman School of Music and I later became his student. I remember the first summer at which there was a student symposium of orchestral compositions and afterward a post mortem session with the composition faculty. The trio of Bernard Rogers, Henry Cowell and Herbert Elwell could have competed with the Ritz Brothers, for what was to be a rather serious discussion of the works turned out to be quite a session for the punsters. Rogers loved to talk and could expound wisdom and wit with little difficulty. Cowell was a good match and Elwell in his droll way often stole the show.

Bernard Rogers always had much to say and could put down an inferior piece with the most severe sarcasm. On the other hand he was quick to praise a work of merit. Though fellow students had cautioned me that Rogers would not be an easy man with whom to study, I thoroughly enjoyed my association with him and felt that he helped me immeasurably with the orchestral idiom.

Rogers was a humble man who took great interest in his students and in his home life. He was very much interested in art and was himself an amateur painter. In fact he continued to spend a great deal of time with his oils as a relaxing hobby. He also loved history and the arts of China and Japan which inspired two sets of 'Japanese Dances.'

Our class was on hand when he reached his 70th birthday and we planned a little party for him in class. He was very touched by this as he was by the special program held in his honor at the time of his retirement, May 21, 1967.

A performance by students and faculty was given of Roger's *Trio for Violin, Viola and Cello;* the *Sonata for Violin;* and his delightful fantasy on the children's tale 'The Musicians of Bremen.' This last work possesses the color, the sparkle, and humor that were truly Bernard Rogers. He died in Rochester on May 24, 1968.

Rochester composer David Diamond said: 'His music is conceived in great intimacy, worked over and molded with loving care. There is no pedantry in his music. Simplicity was Rogers' chief virtue and he was most successful as a miniaturist.'[5]

Rogers once quoted Clifton Fadiman who said, 'To inform is a good thing, to inflame is better.' I think he took this to heart as one can see from the names of a few of his successful students: Peter Mennin, Robert Ward, David Diamond, Gardner Read, Russell Smith, Burrill Phillips and Vladimir Ussachevsky.

A committee of Eastman School faculty members have established the Bernard Rogers Memorial Award to be granted annually to a talented undergraduate student and this will perpetuate the name of the composer who gave so much to so many students and to the Eastman School of Music.

[1] Leedy, Denoe, 'Arthur Shepherd.' *Modern Music,* Vol. XVL, No. 2, 1939, p. 88.

[2] Chase, Gilbert, *America's Music,* p. 394.

[3] Newman, William S., 'Arthur Shepherd,' *Musical Quarterly,* April 30, 1950, p. 163.

[4] Leedy, Denoe 'Arthur Shepherd' *Modern Music,* Vol. XVI, No. 2 1939, p. 88.

[5] Diamond, David. 'Bernard Rogers,' *Music Quarterly,* April, 1947.

BERNARD ROGERS
classroom notes

Bernard Rogers was warm and friendly in personality and essentially a very unassuming man. He had a profound knowledge of music and of orchestration, and his Bible, as it were, was the Rimsky-Korsakoff *Principles of Orchestration.* He would often quote or play examples from this book whenever someone did not have something to show him or we might engage in some highly philosophical discussion concerning musical aesthetics. He took a genuine interest in his students and their work and had a progressive and forward outlook.

Rogers, like Cowell, had a rare ability to make puns and he could whither a student with a single quip after looking over his music. One student was describing his piece which depicted vast verdant fields. After looking at the music for a few moments Rogers said, 'Yes, corn fields.' Another student was describing his work which was like a ferris wheel and he made circles in the air in clockwise fashion. Rogers contemplated this for a moment and said, 'Yes, but yours goes this way' and he made motions in counter clockwise fashion. His one plea when seeing an overly black score was for a few white notes.

He always spoke softly in almost a sotto voice in such a manner that you might think that he didn't care, but he did and always was aware of everything that was going on. During one class he closed the lid of the upright piano in his room and said that it had heard enough bad notes for one day. He was very keen on how we had orchestrated our ideas and was quick to pick a flaw in the registration or the choice of a particular instrument for a passage.

My notes include such commands as: 'Check yourself — evaluate what you do. Is there enough bass? Am I overworking my idea? Have I overworked the strings? Do I have too many ideas going on at one time? What is the best instrument for this part?' We were encouraged to ask ourselves these questions while working.

Rogers felt that his task was to free the student from the grip of habit. He observed that Michaelangelo said that, 'Perfection is the result of an infinite number of trifles, but that perfection is no trifle.'

He said that the composers' world is in ferment. Which way? Right, center or left? Impulse or patience? In his teaching he dwelt on the power of design; the ideal of form, the importance of the 'total.' Yet, he also wanted us to know that everything was meaningful; that a single line, a rhythm, can make or enhance the beauty of a thought. He pointed out the seething crescendos on *B* natural in 'Wozzeck' of Berg.

Contentment, blissful as it seems to the shallow, is fatal to the artist. To be eternally dissatisfied is to be rich in life, 'life is the blood of art.' This mistake that most of us make, which is so natural, is to allow the saving spirit of self-criticism, which he called dissatisfaction, to sink to the plane of pessimism. He said, 'It has no place in life, no place in art.'

These are a few of the words of wisdom dropped from his lips in class: 'It's a nice theme; I wish you had written it.' 'An unwritten composition is like an unborn baby — they're both dependent dictators.' 'Modesty is the fig-leaf of mediocrity.' 'Return to tonality — sometimes a sort of death-bed repentance.' 'If you must make mistakes, try not to make them in the brass.' About a student's excesses in composing: 'You'd better go to confession.'

'Persevere, cultivate taste and study the best masters tirelessly and with love. In them you will find something of yourself for they are universal. In art there is no quick, easy way. Make your studies musical, do nothing without enthusiasm — even when working a simple harmony exercise. It is an attribute which grows.' Rogers, like Schumann, was full of profound aphorisms.

We were not to fall in love with our ideas and gain a narcissus complex but to go along with the idea not stopping every few bars to analyze. When discussing Strauss he said, 'Take the horn theme from Strauss' *Don Juan* as a characteristic example of typical brass music. (Plays the theme.) Of course, Strauss was born in the horn. (Pause.) Even though that does seem inconceivable.'

To orchestrate is to paint,' he would say. Don't just transfer your sketch to the score but the score is the pallette at which you paint. Let the whole idea of orchestration be a creative process. For instance, consider the bass as an instrument of drama. The bass in the deep register along with flutes can provide a new dimension to your music. The small drum is clearer in effect than the large one. The larger drums add a sense of mystery to the orchestra. He advocated the glockenspiel touch with a knitting needle as well as small sticks on the drum. The triangle and kettle drum in extreme ranges produce a good effect. As one can see from these observations Bernard Rogers was tremendously interested in color.

These and many other ideas he was constantly presenting in class. 'The horns cannot repeat too fast and the trumpets are often disappointing in performance. Give the string choir the bulk of the work for too much wind is wearisome. For rapid tonguing in winds, breath pauses are necessary.' He reminded us that practically the entire range of the piano is covered by woodwinds and strings.

In starting a piece he suggested that we practice writing fugue subjects and that we employ the Beethoven sketch book technique. Write down ideas as they come no matter how crude they may be. Be daring and future in your thinking. The first bar of a work must capture the audience. The initial idea should convey the thought. Don't change from one idea to another. Let the form grow out of the idea instead of always starting with a preconceived form. Put down the essentials in the first sketch, maybe only two voices. Do include tempo and dynamic marks. Know what is happening and what you are doing. Watch habits — whatever they may be, to avoid repeating yourself. Note random ideas as they come. Avoid too much tritone if you are using a row technique. When tonality is abandoned, something as good must take its place (a repeated sound, a rhythmic pattern, vitality, etc.). Don't be afraid to discard a bad idea. The waste basket is your best friend. Let the idea set awhile and don't always take the first solution. He always said, 'Don't try to express too little or too much. You can make much out of little.' This he proved to good effect in his own writing.

Be sure that the idiom in which you write best expresses you and watch that you don't have too many ideas. He might say, 'Don't use all your dissonance in the first five bars, call your shots. Keep some of your ammunition for later.'

Remember the doubling of the strings at the octave gives a big sound whereas the unison doubling of strings gives strength. Use the strings for they are the basis of the orchestra. Let violas or celli carry little figures. Sometimes isolate the second or third stands, too.

We were always encouraged to study scores to see what another composer might have done under similar circumstances. 'In writing a concerto make the cadenza bold and free, and try to get the spirit of the instrument for which you are writing so that it feels like an improvisation.'

Bernard Rogers also suggested that we look into the humor in music. He pointed out that everything does not have to be profound or soul searching; levity is good, too. He said, 'A scherzo has the implication of a joke; not all jokes are sad; only other people's.' His *Musicians of Bremen* exhibits this lighter side.

In choral writing he suggested our using for reference the text *Choral Technique* by Archibald T. Davison. He took the architectural approach and always wanted us to know our plan for what we were doing. Variation form is a growth form which comes out of itself and is not just a string of pearls. Consistently sounding the theme is not necessary. Take some harmony, a fragment or rhythmic device and elaborate on it in the form of a character variation. One element should be constant. In this way it unifies.

He was very fond of Moussorgsky, whom he thought to be a diamond in the rough, and he composed a very successful *Variations for Orchestra* based on a Moussorgsky melody. This was recorded by the Rochester Philharmonic Orchestra under Theodore Bloomfield.

His sound advice for orchestrating was, when you have an instrument taking a high note — support it with another for security's sake. The tam tam and low harp give an interesting sound as do the bass drum and tam tam. The triangle and kettle drum are good in the extreme range. All instruments in the low register and dark strings offer variety dynamically.

'Work as much as you can away from an instrument. Economy lies at the basis of the best art. Listen to music with your mind as well as with your heart. Do not be influenced by fads. Be natural. If your music is good it will make its way. Believe in yourself.' These are profound words spoken by a great man, a great musician, and a real friend.

THREE JAPANESE DANCES
by Bernard Rogers

The *Three Japanese Dances* were composed for orchestra in 1933 and recast stunningly twenty years later for wind ensemble and recorded for Mercury Records by the Eastman Wind Ensemble under Frederick Fennell. Bernard Rogers had said the following of the music: 'Two aspects of Oriental expression have held a strong appeal for me: The Bible; and the arts of China and Japan. The latter arises from my response to the art of Japanese wood block masters, particularly Hiroshige, Hokusai and Sharaku. There are no actual pictorial models. The three pieces are merely acts of fancy.'

The work employs the pentatonic scale, much repetition of motives, a large battery of percussion instruments and a mezzo-soprano voice which sings a solo in the second movement. The list of percussion instruments employed is as follows: snare drum, tenor drum, bass drum, xylophone, glockenspiel, fish-head (piccolo woodblock), antique cymbals, large cymbals, small cymbals, suspended cymbal, small gong, deep gong, tubular bell, Indian tom tom, vibraphone, Chinese drum and temple block.

The first section entitled *Dance with Pennons* is marked 'giocoso' and the opening sound is one of tinkling bells and cymbals depicting young girls weaving to and fro casting ribbons of silk. The use of the glockenspiel, xylophone, antique cymbals, celeste, piano and harp provide an exotic coloring. The opening six measure introduction employs these motives:

The main theme is stated by piccolo, oboe and glockenspiel and the above motives are repeated over and over in the above and other instruments. Rogers often uses just two celli from the section. The use of the harmon mute for trumpet and specific indication for percussion is a Rogers trademark.

Main theme:

pp   staccato

After a complete statement of the theme it is then heard again up a major second and with a change of direction. The flutes have counter motives in sixteenth notes. The *B* theme which is in contrast is given out in flute and English horn and then in piccolo, clarinet and celeste. There is more fragmentation of thematic material and a harp glissando leads into a return of the *A* theme, this time beginning a perfect fourth higher in pizzicato violins and trumpets while the flute and piccolo trill alternately. Another appearance occurs in harp and trumpets as the oboes trill and the strings introduce a fanfare-like figure and motives continue in glockenspiel and piano. Another upward harp glissando returns the *A* theme in piccolo and violin I with the piano providing a counterpoint. This group is answered by harp, glockenspiel and English horn and then just glockenspiel and harp as the score becomes sparse and we have a descending scale comprised of notes from the theme in consecutive order in clarinet and violins I and II. The movement ends pianissimo with strings, piano, flute, and harp. At the end the tubular chimes are struck with a triangle stick and the small cymbal is rubbed with a wire brush. It closes on a *F#* sonority similar to the beginning. The *C#* and *B* in the harp come right from the first measure in the bass motive.

Bernard Rogers was a colorist and a successful miniaturist and had a great ear for striking sonorities and the coupling of the right instruments together to obtain them. His architectural background is evident in his works that always have formal clarity but are never stereotyped. The tripartite form predominates here and in the second movement.

The second movement *Mourning Dance* employs a singing solo voice for the central episode. Roger says, 'The dancer is clad in white (the color of mourning).' An elaborate group of percussion instruments combines in a complex bell sonority against a primitive motive sounded by alto flute and bass flute in free meter. It consists of changing colors over a pedal of *E* as a kind of *klangfarben* melody.

The instruments play. In the middle section the voice sings a poem by John Masefield from his Japanese drama 'The Faithful.' Then there is a return to the instruments. This last section is atmospheric and moving.

The third movement *Dance with Swords* is suggested by the violent, distorted actor portraits of Sharaku. The music is fiercely rhythmic, propelled by thrusting rhythms and highly colored percussion.

Bernard Rogers has an individual way of treating form as in the rondo-like structure of the third movement. The themes are motivically derived from the opening notes of the timpani. It is interesting to observe how small figures of rhythms grow and expand into one large formal design. The life blood of a Rogers work is always dependent upon a very extensive though simple use of percussion.

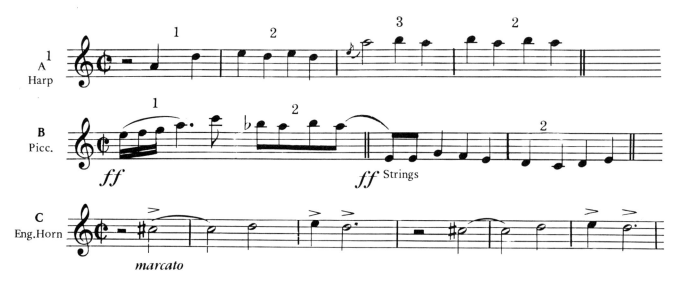

I have quoted from the various themes to show their derivation. The interval of the fourth and its inversion together with the second seems to predominate the texture. We see the use of tremolando and pizzicato in the strings and the rather uncommon use of the hat muted trombone. There is a big build up before letter *K* to a climax on the note *D*. This note is a kind of pivotal note in the piece in that the beginning commenced with the interval (D-A).

The final statement of the theme in piccolo, flute and glockenspiel is answered in canon by contra bassoon, tuba, and piano. There is a stringendo coda with considerable excitement developed by rolls in snare, timpani, and tenor drum against long notes in low winds, horns and low strings. Motivic movement in high strings and winds builds to a big climax with a piano glissando, a cymbal crash and a sustained tone cluster in the piano at the end.

The core of Rogers' vision is always drama. I think with Bernard Rogers' music you are not so impressed by a tune or melody as you are by the over-all sound and atmosphere he creates. It is a wonderful example of what one can do with simple means. The superb working out of his ideas orchestrally, and his consummate craft shine through in everything he did. He was able to capture a mood, an expression, a feeling that makes his music unique.

THE MUSIC OF BERNARD ROGERS

Date	ORCHESTRA	Publisher
1918	To the Fallen	
1922	Overture to 'The Faithful'	
1924	In the Gold Room	
1925	Fuji in the Sunset Glow	
1925	Prelude to 'Hamlet'	R Elkan-Vogel
1933	Three Japanese Dances	P Theodore Presser
1937	The Supper at Emmaus	R Elkan-Vogel
1939	The Song of the Nightingale (Suite)	R Elkan-Vogel
1939	The Colors of War	R Elkan-Vogel
1940	The Dance of Salome	R Elkan-Vogel
1942	The Sailors of Toulon	R Elkan-Vogel
1943	Invasion (Commissioned by League of Composers)	R Elkan-Vogel
1944	Anzacs	R Elkan-Vogel
1945	Elegy, To the Memory of Franklin D. Roosevelt	P Elkan-Vogel
1946	Amphitryon Overture (Commissioned by Juilliard School of Music)	
1951	The Colors of Youth (Commissioned by the Detroit YMCA for their Centennial)	
1953	Dance Scenes (Commissioned by Louisville Orchestra)	R Southern Music
1960	Variations on a song by Moussorgsky (Commissioned by Ford Foundation)	P Theodore Presser
1961	New Japanese Dances (Commissioned by Columbus, Ohio Symphony)	R Theodore Presser
1967	Apparitions	R MCA Music (Belwin Mills)

SYMPHONIES

1926	No. 1 'Adonais'	R Elkan-Vogel
1928	No. 2 in A flat	R Elkan-Vogel
1936	No. 3 'On a Thanksgiving Song'	R Elkan-Vogel
1940	No. 4 in g minor	R Southern Music
1959	No. 5 'Africa'	R Theodore Presser

SMALL ORCHESTRA

	Five Norwegian Folk Songs (After Grieg) Rhapsody Nocturne	
1922	Soliloquy for Flute and Strings No. 1	P Carl Fischer
1924	Pastorale for 11 instruments	
1936	Once Upon a Time	P E.F. Kalmus
1937	Fantasy for Flute, Viola and Strings	R Elkan-Vogel
1938	Soliloquy for Bassoon and Strings (No. 2)	P Elkan-Vogel
1940	The Plains (Commissioned by the League of Composers)	R Elkan-Vogel
1944	Characters from Hans Christian Anderson (Commissioned by WHAM Radio, Rochester)	P Elkan-Vogel
1947	Elegy for Small Orchestra (From Symphony No. 3)	R Elkan-Vogel
1949	The Silver World	P Southern Music
1952	Fantasy for French Horn, Timpani and Strings	P Theodore Presser
1961	Allegory (Commissioned by Edward Benjamin)	R Theodore Presser
1966	Pastorale Mistico (Prelude to the Passion)	

TRANSCRIPTIONS

Three Fold-Songs for Strings	
The Farewell of Dido (Purcell)	P Rochester Music
Orchestra, Small Orchestra	Pub.
Three Japanese Dances for Wind Ensemble	P Theodore Presser
Tribal Drums (2nd movement of Africa	P Theodore Presser
Symphony for wind ensemble)	
Concerto in C for Two Trumpets (Vivaldi)	R C.F. Peters
(For wind ensemble, commissioned by	
American Wind Symphony)	
Concerto for Oboe, op. 30 No. 1 (Vivaldi)	R C.F. Peters
(Commissioned by the American Wind Symphony)	
Concerto grosso for four choirs (Stelsel)	R C.F. Peters
(Commissioned by American Wind Symphony)	
Apparitions for Wind Ensemble	P MCA Music
	(Belwin Mills)

SONGS

The Blood-Red Way (Lillian Soskin)
How do I Love Thee? (Elizabeth Barrett Browning)
The Falling of the Leaves (Wm. Butler Yeats)
I Saw the Marsh (from the Chinese) Helen Waddell
At Dusk (Lillian Rogers)
In the Forest (Oscar Wilde)
Asano's Death Song (The Faithful) John Masefield
Trade Winds (John Masefield)
The White Peace (Fiona McLeod)
At Sunset (Wm. McLeary Curtis)
The Roadside Fire (Lillian Rogers)
In the Gold Room (Oscar Wilde)

PIANO, ORGAN, MARIMBA, FLUTE

1913	Albumblatt (Piano)	
1940	Sacred Dance (Piano)	
1956	Mirage (marimba)	P Southern Music
1964	Study (Piccolo or Flute)	P Rochester Music
		Pub.
	Three Pieces for Organ	P C.F. Peters
	Miniature Suite for Organ	P Theodore Presser
	Second Suite for Organ	P Theodore Presser

CHAMBER MUSIC

1913	Elegy for Cello and Piano
1918	Mood (Violin, Cello, Piano) String Quartet No. 1 Free Variations and Fugue for String Quartet
1925	String Quartet No. 2 in d minor
1937	Untitled (Percussion and two Pianos)
1950	The Silver World for Flute, Oboe, Strings

1953	Trio — Violin, Viola, Cello (Commissioned by Koussevitsky Foundation)	P Southern Music
1959	Ballade (Bassoon, Viola, Piano) (Commissioned by University of Kansas)	
1962	Sonata for Violin and Piano (Commissioned by American String Society of Cleveland, Ohio)	P Theodore Presser

SMALLER WORKS FOR CHORUS

1945	Psalm 99 (Biblical text) STATE Organ Response to Silent Prayer (Biblical) (Commissioned by Temple Emmanual of NYC)	
1955	Hear my Prayer, O God (Biblical) SATB, Sop. Solo Organ	P Theodore Presser
1963	Psalm 18 TTBB, Piano (Commissioned by University of Rochester Men's Glee Club)	P Theodore Presser
	Psalm 89, Lord God of Hosts SATB Bar. solo Piano	P Theodore Presser
1965	Faery Song (John Keats) SSAA, A Cappela	P Theodore Presser
1967*	Dirge for Two Veterans (Walt Whitman) (SATB, Piano)	P Theodore Presser
1968*	Psalm 114 (Biblical) SATB Piano	P Theodore Presser

*Versions for strings and piano by Charles Fussell

CHORUS AND ORCHESTRA

1929	The Raising of Lazarus (Lillian Rogers)	
1931	The Exodus (Charles Rodda)	
1942	The Passion (Charles Rodda)	P Elkan-Vogel

1947	A Letter from Pete (Walt Whitman)	P Southern Music
	(Commissioned by the Jewish Fold Choir	
	of Toronto)	
1950	The Prophet Isaiah (Biblical)	P Southern Music
1964	The Light of Man (Biblical)	P Theodore Presser
	(Commissioned by Methodist Board of Education)	

WORKS WITH NARRATOR OR SOLOISTS

Buona Note Tenor and Orchestra
Alladin (Dramatic Scene) Tenor, Bass, Orchestra

1927	Arab Love Songs — Soprano and Orchestra	
1948	Horse Opera (Text by Martha Keller)	
	Narrator and Orchestra	
1951	Leaves from the Tale of Pinocchio	P Southern Music
	(Narrator and Chamber Orchestra)	
	Psalm 68 (Baritone and Orchestra)	P Southern Music
	(Piano reduction)	
1952	Portrait (Violin and Orchestra)	P Theodore Presser
	(Piano reduction*)	
1958	The Musicians of Bremen	P Theodore Presser
	(Narrator and 13 instruments)	
1965	Aladdin — Narrator and Wind Ensemble	R C.F. Peters
	(Commissioned by American Wind Symphony)	

OPERAS

1922	Deirde (One-act, Piano version only)	
1931	The Marriage of Aude (Charles Rodda)	
1944	The Warrior (Norman Corwin)	
	(Commissioned by the League of Composers	
	and CBS Radio)	
	(Premiered Metropolitan Opera,	
	January 11, 1947)	
1950	The Veil (Robert Lawrence)	R Southern Music
1954	The Nightingale (Composer)	R Southern Music

R. Rental
P. Published

ARTICLES BY AND ABOUT BERNARD ROGERS

Art of Orchestration– Eastman School of Music Series
    published by New York Appleton-Century Crofts. 1951
    reprinted 1970 in Westport, Connecticut

The Composer's Point of View–edited by Robert Hines
    University of Oklahoma Press, 1963
    article, 'The Passion' by Bernard Rogers

Musical America, articles and editorials, 1913-1924.

Modern Music: 1944, Vol. XXI No. 4, p. 246.
                   1944, Vol. XXII No. 2, p. 45.
                   1945, Vol. XXII No. 4, p. 262

Spellbound in Darkness, George Pratt. p. 358.

HENRY COWELL

HENRY COWELL
1896-1965
a short biography

Menlo Park, California was the birthplace of Henry Cowell, who was born on March 11, 1896. His mother, Clarissa Bethshua, was a native of Massachusetts, but subsequently grew up in Amity, Iowa. Here she established her independence at an early age, standing up in church when she was seventeen to declare herself an unbeliever.

As a child young Henry was particularly sensititive to the sounds he heard all around him and tried to devise melodies which these sounds could be translated into music. The earliest connection of Cowell with music dates from the end of 1902 when he began to take violin lessons from Henry Holmes, a septuagenarian Englishman. Two years after lessons were begun he appeared in recital but was soon forced by illness to abandon the violin for composition. When he was six he and his mother moved to a house on Laguna Street, near the Oriental district of San Francisco.

After the great earthquake in San Francisco in 1906, Clarissa was determined to move again. She was a writer but earned little from her work. She took Henry with her to Kansas, Oklahome, Iowa and finally in 1908 to New York City where she hoped to seek her fortune. It was in New York that Cowell began what he considered to be his first serious attempts at composition. At the age of 11 he began an opera based on Longfellow's *Golden Legend* but it was never finished. The melody from it, however, was used later for his piano piece *Antimony.*

Although Cowell suffered much from poor health, he attended the local school sporadically and the resulting diploma from the third grade was his first and last scholastic document until his Honorary Doctorates from Wilmington College in 1954 and Monmouth College in 1953.

Cowell's father married and divorced several times. To make matters worse his mother was not in good health, so when they moved back to Menlo Park young Henry took jobs as janitor, cleaner and collector of wild plants and mushrooms to help the family.

Before the age of 14 he had saved $60.00 to buy himself a piano. He was given lessons in return for gardening, and he began to compose short pieces. In 1911 he was introduced to a Mrs. Ellen Veblen who became a close and valuable friend. The San Francisco Music Club sponsored Cowell in a public concert March 11, 1912. In the fall of 1914 he began music study at the University of California at Berkeley where he came under the influence of Charles Seeger.

During World War I Cowell enlisted for the duration and served for one year as cook and bandmaster. Following this he had two years of study at the Institute of Musical Art in New York then under the direction of Frank Damrosch.

In 1912 he made a formal debut as performer of his own compositions. He made an extended concert tour of Europe playing only his own piano pieces. His first Berlin appearance was arranged by pianist Artur Schnabel, and Bartok managed one of Cowell's first Paris performances where he met Stravinsky and Ravel. Schoenberg invited him to play his music for his composition class. In 1922 Breitkopf and Hartel published a number of his piano pieces: *Tiger* and *The Lilt of the Reel.* He made coast to coast tours in the United States from 1924-1935.

In 1927 Henry Cowell founded the quarterly *New Music* which was to publish some of the most important music of its times, and the following year he joined the faculty of the New School for Social Research in New York. He was most active in arranging concerts, performing and lecturing.

In collaboration with Seeger, Yasser, Kinkeldey and Schillinger he founded the New York Musicological Society in 1931. He visited Europe in the same year on a Guggenheim Fellowship and studied there with Erich von Hornbostel, ethnomusicologist. Two years earlier his book *New Musical Resources* had been accepted by Knopf, Inc. His next book *American Composers on American Music* — symposium, was published in 1933 by Stanford University Press.

In 1941 Cowell married Sidney Robertson, whom he had known before the war. Then he returned to the New School of Social Research and was appointed adjunct Professor at Columbia University. He also offered courses at Stanford University, Mills College and the U.C.L.A. Extension Division.

After the Second World War he was a music consultant and chief music editor to the Office of War Information in charge of short wave broadcasts. In 1948 he received an award from the Academy of Arts and Letters in recognition of his service to American music. He became a member of that organization in 1951 and Vice President in 1961. In 1955 Oxford University Press published Sidney and Henry Cowell's book *Charles Ives and His Music.*

In 1956 he was given a Rockefeller grant in order to spread knowledge of American music and to study the musical situation in various foreign lands. It was a dual task for which no one was better qualified. On this tour, accompanied by his wife, he visited his ancestral country, Ireland, and then traveled throughout Europe and the Middle East spending over two months as the guest of Teheran Radio. He then proceeded to India and Japan, giving concerts and lectures wherever he went.

During the summers of 1962 and 1963, Cowell taught at the Eastman School of Music in Rochester, and it was here as a member of his composition class that I first made his acquaintance. Unlike most professors, he lived with the students in the dormitory, so it was possible to have friendly chats with him at breakfast and supper which were always full of good laughs because of his puckish humor and constant puns. In the evenings he would play bridge with a group of students or demonstrate the playing of his piano pieces which he loved to do. While living in the dormitory he composed one of the concertos for the Japanese koto, a harp-like instrument with thirteen silk strings tuned over movable bridges. He was completely devoid of any self importance. Cowell thoroughly enjoyed the company of the students and was vitally interested in whatever was going on.

That first summer the celebrated saxophonist Sigurd Rascher was at the Eastman School of Music. Cowell became fascinated with the saxophone and wrote a special work, *Aria and Scherzo* for alto saxophone and piano which was premiered there. Mr. Rascher also had with him a bass saxophone which is practically a museum piece. It has approximately an octave range and a sound similar to the contra-bassoon. Cowell composed a short piece for this instrument, too.

There were many students there that summer from Formosa and Japan who came especially to study with Cowell. At the end of July a picnic was held at the home of one of the students and Cowell was invited. We all brought along tapes of previous performances of our works, and he played for us the recording of his orchestral piece, *Music, 1957,* which is lively and employs brake drums in the percussion section. The Eastman Chamber Orchestra performed his *Madras Symphony* no. 13 which utilizes Indian ragas and makes use of a large battery of percussion.

Following the summer of 1963 our paths did not cross again although I kept in touch with him at his New York apartment and his country home in Shady, New York. His answers to my letters were always on Japanese rice paper. Cowell lectured in Germany during the fall and winter of 1963.

In 1965 I suggested to the Board of our Rocky River Chamber Music Society that we bring Henry Cowell to our community to give a performance. Due to my being in residence at Rochester that year, I had to drive West for the performance, but I wouldn't have missed it for anything. He gave a program entitled 'The Autobiography of a Composer' and was introduced by composer-friend Herbert Elwell. He played some of his piano music and also played a tape of his Symphony no. 16 'The Icelandic,' and humorously reminisced about his experiences.

I believe this perhaps was one of Cowell's last public appearances. It was an unforgettable evening the memory of which I shall always treasure. The whole audience felt this, too, I am sure. This concert was in April, 1965 and on December 12 of the same year Cowell died at his secluded home in the Catskills.

Nicolas Slonimsky, conductor, author, composer, said of Cowell: 'It is rare to find a crusader in a big cause whose intellect is as strong as his battle axe. Not all crusaders are more interested in their cause than in themselves. Henry Cowell is the exception who possesses all of these qualities. He would not be himself if he did not follow the path of most resistance.'

HENRY COWELL
classroom notes on composition

Henry Cowell was one of the great trail blazers in the field of sound with his infamous tone clusters or secundal chords as he most recently preferred to call them. Cowell was a breath of fresh air as a teacher for he was completely devoid of any trace of academicism — in fact, he was apt to be quite lax in this respect. Classes took on an informal air as he would relate anecdotes from his past experiences or look at your scores cross-legged, away from the piano. He claimed that the piano just cluttered up his room and that he had long trained himself to hear and write without it.

Before class if you happened to arrive early, you might find him asleep on the floor on an Indian mat, as he always took an afternoon siesta. Like Bernard Rogers he was a great punster and was full of Irish humor. Serial music he felt was something that the Post Division of General Foods might be interested in to promote breakfast cereals. He was quite proud of the fact that when he played his own music in London in 1920's that *The Times* headline read: 'The Loudest Pianist in the World.'

He would eagerly play you some of his famous piano compositions such as the *The Tides of Manaunaun* or the *Aeolian Harp* and he admitted his *Tiger* to be one of the wildest in captivity. He also spoke of his invention the *Rhythmicon* which was a joint effort of his and Theremin, the Russian scientist. The *Theremin,* bearing the name of its inventor, was one of the first electronic instruments to attract public attention. This instrument uses a radio-frequency beat system of tone generation based on the interference between the outputs of two oscillators. One oscillator operates at a fixed frequency and the other at varying frequencies determined by the proximity of the player's hand to a short rod antenna, which is charged with alternating current from the second oscillator. The difference between the frequencies of the two oscillators produces a 'beat,' i.e., a third frequency, which is the audio-frequency that operates the loudspeaker. The volume of sound is controlled in a similar manner by the player's other hand.[1]

The *Rhythmicon,* on the other hand, is really a new variety of percussion instrument with a two manual keyboard in which the tones are produced by rotating discs inserted between a light source and photo electric cell. It was used to illustrate the performance of complex cross rhythms — four against three, or nine against five. He told us that there were two of these instruments, the one was thrown out because the caretakers at Columbia University thought it was a pile of junk, the other remained in the studio of Joseph Schillinger and is now in New York Museum of Natural History.

A good deal of class time was spent in talking about the percussion section which interested Cowell greatly. He had used pyrex bowls in one of his scores and he said that he always enclosed a note in the bottom: 'Do not hit too hard as it might break.' In our piece he encouraged us to indicate specific percussion in the score and to especially watch our notation. He said, 'A percussion piece has form through rhythm and in the tone color of the instruments.'

Cowell said also that he learned to improve his calligraphy when one of his symphonies was to be played by Koussevitzky and he refused to rehearse it as he could not read it. At that point Henry Cowell hired the copying done professionally and later received an enormous bill into the thousands of dollars for the job. In order to repay this he had to take out several loans. The moral of the story was that his calligraphy improved 90% immediately.

The following were certain points mentioned in class in connection with writing for orchestra: '*Write harmonics* where you want them to sound. Indicate the principal part for the string players by means of a bracket. For vivid string writing write for the outside strings of the instrument. Scoring a high part on a lower string gives brightness. As you increase in dynamics write fewer notes to the bow.'

'Indicate the end of trills with two grace notes for the termination so that they come together. Don't make the climax in the orchestra too high in range — the horns are best for climax — trumpets are not as effective. They are too high. From low to high in the scale reinforce the clarinet in the high range with another instrument. Accents all belong above the staff. Brass with strings is not so good. The sound is too thick. The horns blend with everything but brass and winds rarely do. Use chromatic spelling if you go from *F* double sharp to *G* or from *G* to *F#.*

In writing a piece it is a good idea to introduce new material toward the end just as you would expect things to stop. Mozart and Beethoven did. In spelling either spell chordally so it makes a chord or polyphonically by line. Try something in four part writing with secundal harmony. Sustain some chords and let others move in oblique motion. Practice dissonant counterpoint in two parts after selecting a row or atonal scale.'

Reference was made by Cowell to Tebor Serly who has written a treatise regarding the percussive effects on the strings. He also made mention of William Malm of East Lansing, who is an authority on Japanese music. He pointed out that the least explored Oriental music was that of Persia. He said, 'If you want to study harmony or chords, this is the specialty of the Western world of music. If you want to study melody and rhythm, you go to India because they know a great deal more about these as a study than we do in the Western world.'

We were told that a child in India learns the fundamental scales and there are seventy-two of them. He first learns these before being permitted to make variations. In the Madras

Academy of India, he said he was shown a volume which looked like our encyclopedia in which there are listed 32,000 varieties of scales. However, no musician could do more than 600 of them. While at the Eastman School of Music one summer, Cowell composed a concerto for the Japanese koto for Kimio Eto, one of the greatest performers on this instrument alive.

We were reminded that secundal chords do not resolve, so that if we wanted a resolution we should build our chords in thirds. The chords in seconds are more fragile as they come from non-fragile overtones. The relationship of tones in the outer octaves are less dissonant. In his *5th Symphony,* the second movement contains tone clusters in canon and harmonic counterpoint in seconds.

Henry Cowell's piano music is a veritable catalogue of the early effects of playing on the strings of the piano and in the use of tone clusters for the hand and forearm on the keyboard. These pieces have become as much a reference for the piano as Bartok's six string quartets have for the strings. His influence in these experiments spread to such composers as Lou Harrison and John Cage, who were former students.

Ever since 1930, Cowell has had a course at the New School for Social Research in New York called 'Music of the World's Peoples.' A large number of his scores represent his intense interest in the field, namely *Homage to Iran* for violin and piano, the *Madras Symphony, Persian Set 1957,* and two concertos for *koto and orchestra.* Cowell became one of the outstanding authorities on Oriental music, and the State Department automatically called on him to represent America when there was a conference in Teheran or Bangkok. He discussed with us the cycle of modes with the fourth step being the principal step and not the fifth in this order: (C-G-D-A-E-B flat-F#). He mentioned how Bartok had visited each village in Hungary which had its own music and modes peculiar to it. He collected all of this music which now comprises a tremendous reference collection.[2]

Henry Cowell told us that he knew Bartok, who once asked him when he was giving concerts in Europe, if he might incorporate some of his tone clusters into his own music. Cowell also studied with Schoenberg and pointed out how in his classes no mention was made of the twelve tone system. The course was devoted to the study of the quartets of Mozart. After six weeks of intensive study Schoenberg said to the class: 'Gentlemen, you now know all you need to know regarding musical composition. Go out and write your own music.'

On the question of a personal or unified style of a composer Henry Cowell said: 'If a man has a distinctive personality of his own, I don't see how he can keep it out of his music. And if he hasn't how can he put it in.'

Cowell was a mover and one of the enliveners of music in our time. He said that composers everywhere today live in the same kind of musical world that he did as a boy in the sense that, like it or not, they are subjected daily to an incredible variety of musical influences.

Nobody any longer can remain safely encapsulated within a single inherited tradition, nor can the most radical musical inventions remain untouched by tradition. 'Never close your ears,' he said. He felt that a composer today must in the course of his training learn to know intimately, to be able to handle and to use acceptably all of the major symphonic techniques, not only modal and baroque counterpoint, but several kinds of dissonant counterpoint and harmony, atonality, polytonality and the twelve tone row, and to understand at least more than one kind of electronic music.

Cowell said: 'I do not see at all why a composer should be limited to the usual material used in Europe for the past 350 years. What interests me is music itself as organized sound, its form, and all the possibilities of a musical idea: to write as beautifully, as warmly and as interestingly as I can.'[3]

[1] *Harvard Dictionary of Music,* 'Electronic Music,' p. 284.
[2] Library of Congress, Washington, D.C.
[3] Thomson, Oscar. *Cyclopedia of Music and Musicians,* 9th ed., 'Henry Cowell' Thomas Scherman, p. 457.

MUSIC FOR PIANO
by Henry Cowell

This collection of piano music includes many of the early pieces that Henry Cowell played on his European tour in the 1920's. The first piece entitled *The Tides of Manaunaun* begins with a long melody similar to an Irish folk song. Cowell was influenced by Irish mythology and folk songs through his friend John Varian and through his parents.

In performance Henry Cowell usually related the story of this piece which concerns *Manaunaun,* the god of motion. Long before the creation he sent forth tremendous tides which swept to and fro through the universe, and rhythmically moved the particles and materials out of which the gods were later to make the suns and worlds. In order to get the feeling of the tides he discovered the tone cluster played with the flat of the hand and with the entire forearm.

The little peasant song in the right hand never loses its diatonic harmony but is transfigured by the addition of ostinato figures. Here we see Cowell putting together disparate elements into a whole. The piece builds to a shattering climax with forearm clusters and it ends quietly as it began.

The following are examples of the tone clusters and how they should be played:

should be played

if sharped # added above cluster it means only black keys are to be played

if natural added above cluster it means only white keys are to be played

forearm, with flat of hand or fist depending upon the length of the cluster

Symbols X and + indicate use of the fist.

Symbols ◇ ♦ ♦ require a silent pressing down and holding down of the key in order that the open string may be subjected to sympathetic vibrations.

Tone cluster in above symbols:

The piece *Fabric* utilizes new notation.

3rd note series — (Triangular shaped notes)

2-3rds note: △   3rd note: △   6th note: ▲

12th note: ▲   24th note: ▲   48th note: ▲

5th note series — (square notes)

4-5th note: ☐   2-5ths note: ☐   5th note: ■

10th note: ■   20th note: ■   40th note: ■

Old Notation   New Notation

In the piece *Aeolian Harp* the keys are silently depressed and the strings of the piano are swept with the fleshy part of the finger nail. Cowell is very explicit as to what he wants and how it is to be obtained. This is a very colorful and imaginative piece.

Henry Cowell was the first American composer ever to visit Russia. In 1928 he gave a series of his own concerts in Moscow and Leningrad and the Moscow State Edition published his famous piece *Tiger* and *The Lilt of the Reel. Tiger* contains some of the Stravinsky influence and even a hint of Schoenberg. Here we see large clusters used to produce mass sonorities, the use of fists to play small fast loud clusters, and the use of several depressed keys for quiet resonance.

All of the pieces are rhapsodic in form and there is little counterpoint except for the little piece, *Two Part Invention in Three Parts.* The rhythm here is fairly uniform and there are motives developed melodically as well as rhythmically. Cowell's pieces are really performers' music and go far in their expansion of instrumental technique.

Tiger

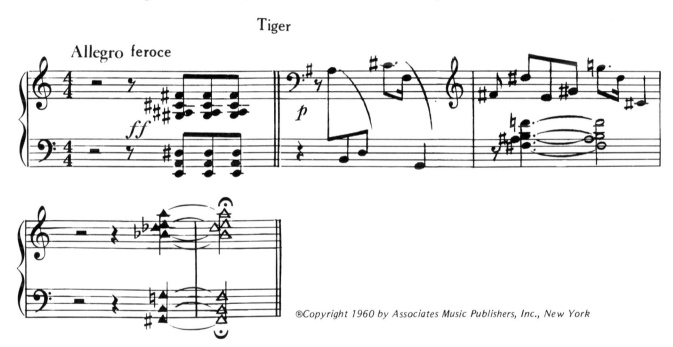

®Copyright 1960 by Associates Music Publishers, Inc., New York

In a later score for ballet, *The Changing Woman,* Cowell employs the largest collection of piano playing techniques ever used by him. The score itself is of little musical interest but the instructions that accompany it are a compendium of devices.

His piece for percussion band entitled *Ostinato Pianissimo* employs 2 piano players for the strings of the piano, 8 rice bowls, xylophone, 2 woodblocks, tambourine (without rattles), 2 bongos, 3 drums, 3 gongs. The form of the work is an ostinato passage which varies in length for each performer, and in accent for the repeats. The string piano part is played by damping the strings which are to be played with the fingers. The sound is most intriguing and the rhythms of great interest.

In Cowell's book *New Musical Resources* he makes a study of overtones, rhythm and dissonant counterpoint, all of which have been developed today but which were regarded in 1912 with some suspicion.

Henry Cowell composed over one thousand or so compositions and about two hundred of them are published. His contributions can be summarized into four categories of musical activity: 1. Experimentation in various sound devices developed in his early piano music; 2. Music on stimulation from Irish ancestry such as the *Gaelic Symphony;* 3. The development of his *Hymn and Fuguing Tunes* in the 1940's from a study of American square note humnology; this also includes Quartets 4 and 5, Symphonies 4, 5, 6, 7, 10, 12 and 15; 4. Music inspired by the Orient and Near Middle East — *The Persian Set* (12 movements), *Ongaku* — two Japanese pieces for orchestra, *Madras Symphony* no. 13, *Homage to Iran, Concertos for koto* (European table harp).

There was never a moment in his life when he devoted himself exclusively to any one thing. It is for this reason that his ideas in his music are always overlapping. His 11th Symphony (The Seven Rituals of Music) is considered by many critics to be his magnum opus. It is explained in the score with the words: 'There are seven rituals of music in the life of man from birth to death.' The symphony opens gently with music for a child asleep, and grows into a celebration of youth and strength. Before the first movement ends there is a moment's premonition of grief, fore-shadowing the lament with which the symphony closes. Percussion consisting of drums, xylophone, cymbals, bowls and piano provide ostinati of varying desities.

A friend of Henry Cowell related a fact which sheds some light on his prolific output. He said, 'Most people who write music want to be composers: Henry just wanted to compose.' This I believe to be the most penetrating observation ever made about Cowell. It explains his unselfed consciousness; his disinclination to be fashionable; his massive output; and it also illumines most of the other problems that he raises.

Though Henry Cowell was primarily an orchestral composer with twenty symphonies to his credit — I feel that he will be remembered more for his early piano music, for such scores as *Ostinato Pianissimo* for percussion, in which his color imagery and experimental nature have free reign, and for his remarkable source book *New Musical Resources* recently reprinted by Something Else Press.

*THE MUSIC OF HENRY COWELL

Since Henry Cowell was a most prolific composer of over one thousand works it is almost impossible to list every one. I have therefore picked out important works to show the tremendous imagination of Cowell through music of varied mediums. His humor comes through in many of the titles.

The last penned composition was a *Trio for Violin, Cello and Piano* (1965) and he had sketches for a 21st Symphony.

Date	ORCHESTRAL WORKS	Recording	Publisher
	20 Symphonies		
1938	No. 2 'Anthropos Symphony'		Peters
1946	No. 4 'Short Symphony'	Mercury	Associated
1948	No. 5	American Recording Soc.	
1952	No. 7	CRI	Associated
	No. 8 'Choral'		
1953	No. 9	Unicorn	Associated
	No. 11 'Seven Rituals of Music'	Columbia	Associated
1958	No. 13 'Madras Symphony'		Peters
1960	No. 15 'Thesis'	Louisville	
1962	No. 16 'Icelandic'	CRI	
1930	Synchrony		Peters
1937	Old American Country Set		Associated
1940	Ancient Desert Drone	Artist	Associated
	Pastorale and Fiddler's Delight		Associated
1941	Tales of our Countryside	Columbia	Associated
1943	Little Concerto for Orchestra/Band		Associated
1948	Saturday Night at the Firehouse	Apa	Associated
1952	Fiddler's Jig	Unicorn	Associated
1953	Rondo for Orchestra		Associated
1955	Ballad for String Orchestra	Unicorn	Associated
1959	Antiphony for two Orchestras		
1960	Chiaroscuro for Orchestra		
1963	Eastern Airlines — Basic 60		
1957	Ongaku-Music of the Art and Science of Sound	Louisville	
1957	Music, 1957	CRI	

HYMN AND FUGUING TUNES 1-17 for String Orchestra

1944	No. 2	Unicorn	Associated
	No. 3		Associated
1945	No. 5	Unicorn	Associated
	No. 5 for full Orchestra		Associated
1955	No. 10		Associated

CONCERTOS

1923	Concerto for Strings and Piano		
1958	Concerto for Percussion and Orchestra		Peters
1960	Concerto for Accordion and Orchestra		
1962	Concerto for Koto and Orchestra		
	Concerto for Harmonica and Orchestra		
1963	Concerto Grosso		
	Concerto for Harp		
1965	Concerto for Koto and Orchestra		

BAND

1939	Celtic Set		G. Schirmer
1942	Little Concerto for Piano and Band		
1944	Hymn and Fuguing Tune No. 1		Leeds
	Animal Magic		

CHAMBER MUSIC

1915-17	'Quartet Romantic'		
	5 String Quartets		
1916	No. 1 'Pedantric'		
1926	No. 2 'Movement for String Quartet'	CRI	
1928	No. 2 'Mosaic'	CRI	
1936	No. 4 'United Quartet for Stringart'	CRI	
1956	No. 5	Columbia	

1915	Sonata for Cello and Piano		
1934	Ostinato Pianissimo	Time	New Music
1936	Vocalise for Strings, Flute, Piano		Peters
1954	Quartet for Flute, Oboe, Cello, Harpsichord		
1957	Persian Set for Flute, Clarinet, Drum, Piano and Strings	CRI	Peters
	Homage to Iran (Violin, Piano and Indian Drum)	CRI	Peters
1961	Air and Scherzo (Saxophone/Piano)		Peters
1962	Quartet for Flute, Oboe, Cello and Harp		
	Trio for Flute, Violin and Harp (Piano)		
	Toccanta for Strings, Flute, Cello, Piano	Columbia	Boosey & Hawkes
1965	Trio for Violin, Cello and Piano	CRI	Peters

OPERA

1947-50	O'Higgins of Chile (never completed)		

PIANO

1923-29	Piano Music		Associated
	The Tides of Manaunaun (1912)		
	Fabric (1917)		
	Exaltation (1919)		
	The Banshee (1925)		
	Aeolin Harp (1923)		
	Episode (1916)		
	Two-Part Invention (1950)		
	Tiger (1928)		
	Advertisement (1914-1959)		
1955	Beethoven Birds, based on 16 motives heard clearly in bird songs while walking along Beethoven's brook in Grinzig.		
	Four Episodes		
	Seven Etudes		
	21 Two-Part Inventions		
	12 Piano Sonatas		

SONGS

1914	Among the Rushes	
	A Baby's Smile	
	And He Will Not Come Again	
	Because the Cat	
	Follow	
1915	Fresh Flowering Sprigs	
	God of the Future	
1916	Christmas Song	
1918	April	
	Saint Agnes Morning	Music Press
1920	The Dream Bridge	
1921	Auntie's Skirts	
	At the Seaside	
1923	Carl's Birthday	
1925	Consecration	
1927	Dust and Flame	
1929	How Old is Song	
1930	Sunset — Rest	New Music
1936	*Vocalise* — Soprano, Flute, Piano	Peters
1938	3 Anti-Modernist Songs	
1946	The Donkey	Music Press
1962	Firelight and Lamp	Peters

CHORUS

1921-22	Atlantis, SAB Soloists, Orchestra (Ballet in 9 movements)	
	Banners, Chorus, Orchestra, Piano, Percussion, String Quartet	
1922	The Building of Bamba, SATBB Soloist, Chorus, Orchestra	
1938	The Coming of Light — Chorus SSAA	Flammer
	Into these Hollows — Chorus SSA	

1943	Fire and Ice — TTBB Band or Orchestra		Boston Music
	American Muse — Chorus, SA Piano		Music Press
1948	Evesong at Brookside		Peer
	Do you Doodle as you Dawdle? Chorus, SSAATTBB, Piano, Drums ad lib		Peters
1954	The Commission 4 Solo Voices / Orchestra		
1955	If He Please Chorus, Orchestra	CRI	Peters
	The Golden Harp — Chorus SATB		
	Granny, Does your Dog Bite? SATB		Presser
	Hamlet: Male Chorus, Orchestra		
	Simple Prayer for Our Day — Chorus SATB		
1956	Septet (SSATB) Madrigal and Vocalize		
1960	Edson Hymns and Fuguing Tunes Chorus, SSAATB, Organ		
1964	Zapadas Sonidos — Chorus SSAATTBB — Tap Dancer for Paul Draper		

BOOKS BY HENRY COWELL

American Composers on American Music
    Stanford University Press
    Oxford University Press, 1933.

Charles Ives and His Music (Sidney and Henry Cowell)
    Oxford University Press, 1955.

New Musical Resources
    Something Else Press, 1969.

*For a complete list of all the music written by Henry Cowell I refer you to the Dissertation 'The Music of Henry Cowell' Cornell University, 1969 by Dr. Jocelyn Godwin.

BIBLIOGRAPHY

A listing of poems used and considered for songs by Arthur Shepherd Dorothy van Stipriaan. University of Utah, Salt Lake City, Utah.

American Composers on American Music — Henry Cowell Stanford University Press, 1933.

Encyclopedia of Music and Musicians — Oscar Thomson

Harvard Dictionary of Music 2nd edition — Willi Apel The Belknap Press of Harvard University, 1969.

Modern Music, 1939 'Arthur Shepherd,' Denoe Leedy

Musical America, Jan. 1962 'Henry Cowell,' Everett Helm

Musical America, Feb. 1947 'Bernard Rogers,' David Diamond

Music Quarterly, April, 1950 'Arthur Shepherd,' William S. Newman

New Musical Resources, Henry Cowell (Something Else Press) 1969

Piano Music, Henry Cowell (Associated Music) score

Perspectives of New Music Fall-Winter 1965, Expressionism and American Music, Spring-Summer 1966, Henry Cowell

Pan Pipes, January, 1966

Three Poems of Robert Liddell Lowe, Herbert Elwell (Fema Music Publishing Co.) score

Three Japanese Dances of Bernard Rogers (Theodore Presser) score

The Art of Orchestration by Bernard Rogers. Appelton, Century, Crofts

Triptych for High Voice and String Quartet, Arthur Shepherd. Theodore Presser score

APPENDIX I

DISCOGRAPHY — Herbert Elwell

The Happy Hypocrite music for the ballet ARS 37 (monaural)
    American REcording Society
    Walter Hendl, conductor

Pastorale for voice and orchestra
    Hallmark Recording CS 1 (monaural)
    Toronto Shyphony Orchestra
    Lois Marshall, soprano

*Suite from *The Happy Hypocrite*
    Epic LC-3819 (monaural)
    Cleveland Pops Orchestra
    Louis Lane, conductor

Concert Suite for Violin and Orchestra
    LOU-593 (monaural)
    Louisville Orchestra
    Robert Whitney, conductor
    Sidney Harth, violin

Four Songs
    CRI- SD-270 (Stereo)
    Maxine Markas, soprano
    Anthony Makas, piano
        I Look Back (Pauline Hanson)
        Wistful (from the Chinese)
        Giorno dei morti (D.H. Lawrence)
        A Child's Grace
        This Glittering Grief (Robert Liddell Lowe)
        The Ouselcock (Shakespeare)

*The monaural recordings may only be available through public or college libraries.

DISCOGRAPHY — Arthur Shepherd

Triptych for High Voice and String Quartet
    Marie Simmelink Kraft, mezzo-soprano
    Walden String Quartet
    American Recording Society ARS 18 (Monaural)

The Old Chisholm Trail from 'Horizons'
    Cleveland Pops Orchestra
    Louis Lane, conductor
    Epic LC 3819 (monaurual)

Songs of Arthur Shepherd published by
     Case-Western Reserve University
     Marie Simmelink Kraft, mezzo-soprano
     Marianne Matousek Mastics, piano (monaural)

*The above recordings are no longer available except through libraries for loan. The last mentioned disc may be obtained by writing Case-Western Reserve University, Cleveland, Ohio 44106, c/o Music House.

DISCOGRAPHY — Bernard Rogers

Apparitions
     Royal Philharmonic Orchestra
     Seymour Lipkin, conductor CRI S-259

Three Japanese Dances
     Eastman Wind Ensemble
     Frederick Fennell, conductor Mer. 90173

Variations on a song by Moussorgsky
     Rochester Symphony Orchestra
     Theodore Bloomfield, conductor CRI-153

Leaves from the Tale of Pinnachio
     American Recording Society Orchestra
     Desto 6424

DISCOGRAPHY — Henry Cowell

Piano Music
     'Episode,' 'Invention,' six ings plus one (1950)
     Rogers — piano
     CRI — S-281

Sinfonietta (1928)
     Louisville Orchestra
     Jorge Mester, conductor
     Lou — S681

Synchrony (1931) *Variations for Orchestra* (1956)
     Polish National Radio Orchestra
     William Strickland, conductor
If He Please (1954)
     Norwegian choir of solo singers and members of
     Oslo Philharmonic Orchestra
     William Strickland, conductor
     CRI — 217 -USD*

Hymn and Fuguing Tunes no. 1–8 (1943–7)
  Louisville Orchestra
  Robert Whitney, conductor
  Lou-S-682

Symphony no. 4 (Short) (1946)
  Eastman Rochester Symphony
  Howard Hanson, conductor
  Mercury MG 50078*

Ballad for String Orchestra (1955)
  F. Charles Adler and Vienna Orchestra
  Society, Unicorn LA-1-11*

Persian Set (1957)
  Leopold Stokowski and members of his Symphony Orchestra
  CRI-114

Music — 1957
  Japan Philharmonic Orchestra
  Akeo Watanabe, conductor
  CRI-132

Ongaku (1957)
  Louisville Orchestra
  Robert Whitney, conductor
  Lou-595

Symphony no. 7 (1952)
  Vienna Symphony Orchestra
  William Strickland, conductor
  CRI-142

Symphony no. 11 (Seven Rituals of Music) 1954
  Louisville Orchestra
  Robert Whitney, conductor
  Columbia ML 5039
  Lou 542-2*

Symphony no. 15 (Thesis) 1961
  Louisville Orchestra
  Robert Whitney, conductor
  Lou 622

Symphony no. 16 (Icelandic) 1962
  Iceland Symphony Orchestra
  William Strickland, conductor
  CRI-179

Ostinato Pianissimo for Percussion Orchestra (1934)
Manhattan Percussion Ensemble
Paul Price, conductor
Time 58000
Main 5011 M 550011**

Quartet no. 5 (1956)
Beaux Arts String Quartet
Columbia MS 6388 ML 5788**

The recordings with no asterisk are all listed in the Fall '72 supplement of Schwann catalogue.

Synchrony, Cleveland Public Library catalogue no. 69-283.
Symphony no. 4, Cleveland Public Library catalogue no. 6-95.
Ballad for String Orchestra, Cleveland Public Library catalogue no. 73-5063, reference.
Symphony no. 11, Cleveland Public Library catalogue no. 70-1566.
**Ostinato Pianissimo* and *Quartet no. 5* are both monaural recordings and no longer listed in Schwann but may be available in music libraries.

APPENDIX II

Reviews from the *Plain Dealer* by Herbert Elwell

SZELL HAZES AUDIENCE — PUTS SPUR TO 'ROMEO'

An all-Tchaikovsky program was presented by the Cleveland Orchestra and George Szell last night at Severance Hall. It began with the *Romeo and Juliet* Overture Fantasie, followed by the Violin Concerto in D major, in which the soloist was Nathan Milstein.

The orchestra had played only a few measures of the overture when Szell stopped, turned to the audience and said: 'I'll give you five minutes to clear your throats.' When he returned to the stage he again turned to the audience and said, **'**We are trying to do our best, won't you try to do likewise and exercise a little self-control and refrain from disturbing the performance?' There was some applause, also a few boos.

After this bit of unpleasantness the program went ahead as scheduled and as expected although it may be doubted whether anybody ever expected Romeo and Juliet to make love at a faster tempo. The orchestra was driven unmercifully at speeds which would certainly be frowned on by traffic officers, if not music critics.

One can condone the urgency which the young Shakespearean lovers must have felt, but what pleasure could they have had at such speed and under such tension? Battles are won by swift strategy and possibly the conductor had uppermost in mind the brawl between the Capulets and the Montagues, but which side was the orchestra on and who won?

One could certainly say that the orchestra was on Szell's side. It had to be, or else, but it is to be doubted whether the members were happy in the act of making music under these circumstances, even though they won a sort of hysterical applause from the audience.

Similarly frenetic, not to say frantic, vehemence was evident in the concerto, where Milstein charged along valiantly at super velocity, and no small degree of what used to be called 'schmalz.' The notes were all there, though it took fast work to count them. And the audience went wild with enthusiasm.

After clearing my throat as quietly as possible, I must say in a whisper that I couldn't buy it. The last half was devoted to the F minor Symphony, no. 4 which an early deadline prevented me from reviewing.

Szell waited some time before appearing after the intermission, in which time there was really a lot of coughing, some of it, one suspects, quite deliberate. Then the audience broke into laughter, the conductor came on and the atmosphere melted into one of friendliness.

From Herbert Elwell's column, May 6, 1962

BERNARD ROGERS LENDS DISTINCTION TO MUSICAL PROGRAMS

Contemporary composers get so little publicity compared to performing artists that the musical scene has become entirely unbalanced. Something should be done to rectify this situation.

One does not begrudge the interpreter his right to prominence. But it should be remembered that if it were not for the composer, the interpreter would have nothing to interpret.

There is one composer, however, about whom a few words should be said at this time. He is Bernard Rogers, since 1929 a faculty member of the Eastman School of Music and widely known as one of the most distinguished composers of our time.

Last week his admirable Trio for strings was heard at the Cleveland Museum of Art in the Music School Settlement's opening concert of the Fourth May Festival of Contemporary Music. This week, Friday night, we shall hear his new Sonata for violin and piano commissioned by the Cleveland Chapter of the Society for Strings, and dedicated to Josef Gingold, who will be heard in the violin part.

One of the most vivid memories of his music heard here is his *Portrait* for violin and orchestra composed for and performed by Josef Gingold at Severance Hall in 1956.

Rogers has to his credit over 60 large works, among them three operas, and four symphonies. His opera *The Warrior* based on the Samson legend, won the Ditson Prize and was produced at the Metropolitan Opera in New York in 1947.

Among the many cantatas he has written is a version of *The Passion* which was once conducted by Robert Shaw. I have heard a recording of this work, which is quite magnificent, and I wonder why Shaw, with the splendid equipment he now has, does not revive it here.

Literally hundreds of students have studied in Rogers' classes at Eastman. They regard him with affection and loyalty, and several of them have risen to high places in the music world.

In spite of the high honors Rogers has received (he is a member of the National Institute of Arts and Letters), he remains a modest person with simple tastes. Although he has reached the retiring age, he still teaches in both winter and summer sessions at Eastman, and he continues to fulfill many commissions.

Rogers is known at Eastman for his spicy wit and his icy irony. But his sarcasm is never intended to be unkind. I would say he is one of the kindest and gentlest persons I ever have known, and I have known him for many years. He is also one of the most fabulous punsters in history, and can keep you laughing until your sides split.

But with all his humor and geniality he appears at times, in his music, as a tragic and lonely figure, one who senses these traits in the American character with deep sensitivity and accuracy. He is a lovable person, but he will fight like a tiger for his convictions, as I well know from arguments I have had with him.

He has no special love for critics, who in some cases probably have done him injustices through ignorance of his aims and unique achievements. But, although I have followed the profession of music critic for many years, we long have been friends, and I hope we always will remain so.

Plain Dealer, May 3, 1961

ALL THAT'S GOULD GLITTERS AT SEVERANCE

The children were crouched about daddy's feet awaiting the usual bedtime story.

'Isn't it a bit late for you kids to be up?' daddy asked. 'But daddy,' they shouted, 'don't you remember you promised to tell us about the concert you went to at Severance Hall last night. Was it full, daddy?'

'Yes, my dears, it was full, and there were some little people like you there. I really should have taken you with me so that some day you could tell your children about this chap, Glenn Gould, just as I am going to tell you about him now. He is an extraordinary musician.'

GOULD IS EVERYTHING

'What sort of a musician, daddy. A singer, a conductor, a pianist?'

'That's just the extraordinary part of it,' exclaimed daddy with some vehemence, 'he's all three put together, and a bit of an acrobat in the bargain, what with the way he twisted his legs, coiled, crouched and sprang at the piano like a wild animal.'

'The singing wasn't quite loud enough so you could hear the words, and you wondered what sort of words he was making up, because there really aren't any words to music like of William Byrd, or Bach's Partita no. 2, Mozart Sonato in C major, Beethoven's Sonta in E major or thatt peculiar Sonato no. 1 of Alban Berg.'

ONE HAND CONDUCTING

'What about his conducting?'

'Well, he did that with only one hand at a time, because you see he had to keep the other on the keyboard to keep the music going, but somehow he managed to do both.'

'Ha, ha, ha,' laughed the children. 'But what was his playing like?'

'I would say,' said father, growing serious, 'that it is extremely romantic, in the finest tradition, and marvelously skillful. It glowed with a sort of diabolic ecstasy.'

'Oh, papa, don't use big words like that,' chorused the children. 'What did you REALLY think of him.'

'I thought,' said father in all solemnity, 'that he is one damned fine pianist.'

June 16, 1963

HAIL VOCALIST MARIE KRAFT AS LEADER IN MUSICAL TASTE

Marie Simmelink Kraft deserves a salute from the musical community for the distinction she has brought to it as a singer and educator. Few persons on the Cleveland scene have contributed more to the cultivation of musical taste.

Her resignation as head of the voice department at the Cleveland Institute of Music was announced with regret last Tuesday by the director, Victor Babin. Her departure from the institute, after twenty-six years on its faculty, leaves a serious void. She became associate head of the voice department in 1945, and head in 1949.

Great as is her loss to the Institute, her leaving far from spells the close of an extremely active career. Those who know Mrs. Kraft's dynamic personality and capacity for work would find it difficult to believe that she intends to rest on her laurels.

The probability is that she will use her newly freed time and energy to broaden the scope of her interests, and remain active in the field of music making. Her enthusiasm for all forms of music has distinguished her as a knowledgeable musician, in contrast to the vocalist who is content with limited specialization.

In addition to her full teaching schedule at the Institute and her annual recitals there, Mrs. Kraft has sung in oratorio, opera and as soloist with numerous symphony orchestras. She has appeared under the baton of Bruno Walter, Leopold Stokowski, George Szell, William Steinberg, Artur Rodzinski, Nikolai Sokoloff, Howard Hanson and others.

Her first appearance in New York was as soloist in the 'Israel Symphony' of Ernest Bloch, under Sokoloff. Memorable successes with Rodzinski were her performances of Ravel's 'Scheherazade' and De Falla's 'El Amor Brujo.' She has sung many times with the Cleveland Orchestra here and on tour.

Perhaps the finest example of her prowess was when she stepped in, at a few hours notice, to sing the solo in Mahler's Fourth Symphony under Walter in 1946. The great conductor expressed delight with her artistry. In 1950 she sang the same solo under Szell at Ann Arbor.

Marie Kraft was born in Cleveland and graduated from Western Reserve University, which last spring awarded her a citation as an outstanding alumna. On July 15, 1962, she lost her husband, Edwin Arthur Kraft, renowned concert organist, and for a half century organist and choirmaster at Trinity Cathedral.

Not the least of Mrs. Kraft's activities, in addition to her devotion to song masters like Schubert, Schumann, Hugo, Wolf, Brahms, Debussy and Faure, is her diligent promotion of contemporary music, much of it home-grown. First performances by dozens of American composers appear on her programs.

She was first to introduce here, and in Oberlin, important new works like Hindemith's cycle 'Marienleben.' She was vocal soloist at the American Music Festival at the Yaddo Foundation in Saratoga Springs in 1952. She sang Arthur Shepherd's 'Trptych' at a festival at Columbia University, and subsequently recorded it, as well as 16 of his songs. She has won complimentary reviews from critics as noted as Paul Hume and the late Olin Downes.

Two things this artist rightly has insisted upon are fine poetry for the songs she selects, and fine accompanists. She demands that the text of a song be as beautiful as the music. With her pianists she shares equal honors.

Among these have been Arthur Loesser and the late Beryl Rubinstein, with whom she presented Faure's 'La Bonne Chanson' at the Museum of Art; also Leonard Shure, with whom she did the two big Schubert cycles, 'Winterreise' and 'Die Schone Muellerin.' And more recently, Marianne Matousek Mastics.

Lastly, in the account of this artist, who in many ways deserves to be compared to some of the greatest, like Maria Freund, Povla Frisch, Eva Gautier and Maggie Teyte, I will throw modesty to the winds and confess that she has been the inspiring interpreter for much of my own music.

She first sang my setting of John Gould Fletcher's 'Blue Symphony' here with the Walden String Quartet. Later she sang it in New York, Washington, D.C., Columbus, Toledo, Rochester, and other places.

She was the first to sing my 'Pastorale' for orchestra and voice, commissioned by Szell and dedicated to her; also my setting of Pauline Hanson's 'The Forever Young,' which she sang under Stokowski in St. Louis.

Cleveland Press Music and Art Section
November, 1949
ARTHUR SHEPHERD WRITES ABOUT SZELL'S CONDUCTING

An invitation to contribute a commentary on Thursday evening's symphony concert comes as a lucky turn that many an attendant at that notable event might envy.

All too seldom in these chaotic days is one reawakened by some faith-renewing experience; some reaffirmation of the eternal verities inherent in great art: This, however, was our happy lot on the occasion of George Szell's Cleveland debut.

What was it in particular, that sent such a thrill of excitement and exaltation through the audience at the conclusion of the 'Pastoral' Symphony? It was nothing less than Beethoven redivivus!

Does this imply that somehow through the years, effective contact with that great soul had been lost? Those of us who date from the days of Nikisch, Gericke, Much, Weingartner and Mahler feel that something like that had happened through the metrically slick or pedestrian performances that have prevailed through recent years. It was no less a celebrity than Maestro Arturo Toscanini who rediscovered the metronome, but fortunately there remain a few regenerate souls like Koussevitzky, Bruno Walter and George Szell who have forgotten that pesky device.

Escapes Metrical Beat

In Mr. Szell one suddenly becomes aware of a conductor who has escaped the dead hand of the 'metrical' beat and who is not content to whip up a neat ensemble through the metronomic line of least resistance in rehearsal. Under his vitalizing baton one becomes aware of the fusion of expressive rhythmic inflection and sensitive phrasing.

What is still more unique, he actually avows and discloses the romantic nuance that is the very life-pulse of every symphonic masterpiece from Beethoven to Sibelius.

Now if there might be designated a symphony, which constitutes the acid test in effective interpretation, it is precisely this Sixth Symphony of Beethoven. It has become almost axiomatic to rate the slow movement 'by the brook' as 'picturesque' but dull. Under Szell's baton it was a poem of sheer loveliness and tranquility. Tempo and rhythmic flow had that inevitable rightness upon which the mood is so subtly dependent. Many a conductor has found the 'storm' episode equally problematical through a seeming inadequacy of instrumentation. Here again, Szell revealed the true eloquence of these pages that moved Berlioz to such rhapsodic commentary.

In addition to an amazing breadth of singing eloquence there was throughout an exceptional harmonic clarity and exquisite balance in the woodwinds that stamped the performance of this symphony as the greatest within memory.

Effective Orchestration

If a renaissance of the romantic spirit be within future possibilities, one may respond all the more sympathetically to the auto-biographical 'Aus mein Leben' of Smetana in Szell's orchestral version. The transcription is highly effective and beneficial to the inner drama and intensity of this work. One carries remembrance of performances in the original quartet setting that invariably sounded strained and unidiomatic.

Even in such an irresistible bravura piece as Strauss' 'Till Eulenspiegel' Szell evinced more concern for dramatic delineation than for too obvious virtuoso display to which we have been accustomed. There was, of course, virtuosity aplenty but it was the virtuosity of 'Till's' gorgeous rogueries and not a batonic by-product.

The response of orchestra and audience alike came as a well earned tribute to a great conductor.

February 1, 1929, Cleveland Press
MASONIC HALL IS FILLED FOR YEHUDI MENUHIN
Child Prodigy, Master Violinist, Delights Audience with Beethoven Concerto
by Arthur Shepherd

Last night's symphony concert must be put down as an extraordinary event on several counts.

The first half of the program was an impressive memorial to the late Mrs. John L. Severance whose name, together with that of her husband, has been, through the past decade, synonomous with the growth and development of the Cleveland Orchestra.

The works chosen specially for this occasion were Schubert's 'Unfinished Symphony' — a favorite of Mrs. Severance's and the Funeral March from Beethoven's 'Eroica' Symphony.

At the close of the latter number, the audience arose in silent tribute to the memory of the much beloved woman.

A record breaking audience turned out to greet Yehudi Menuhin, the astonishing youngster, who has set the country by the ears with his incredible playing.

300 Turned Away

I was told that there were over 300 people turned away from the box office for last night's concert, and that the Friday concert is completely sold out in advance. Thus does curiosity remain as one of the ineradicable traits of the human kind.

In the present instance, curiosity was richly rewarded. Doubtless there were many in last night's audience who had that indescribable thrill of being in on the initial stage of a history-making phenomenon.

Somewhere back along the line I have read that 'genius, like 'the imponderable ether,' is one of the inexplicable mysteries.'

Present indications are that the ether mystery is much nearer solution than that of genius.

An Adorable Boy

When the latter is manifested in the person of an adorable 12-year-old boy like Yehudi Menuhin, one has the hope that it may remain forever unsolved.

There is something infinitely touching to hear the eternal verities of a great classical masterpiece expounded through the priceless heritage of youth.

The thrice astonishing feature of Master Yehudi Menuhin is that he brings one into immediate contact with the larger and deeper aspect of music.

Over and over again in his performance of the Beethoven concerto there was the awareness of true artistic perception, of authentic musicianship.

In addition, there is the fascination of an unaffected and unspoiled child upon whom the gods have smiled and who has fortunately fallen into the hands of masterful and wise guidance.

One may indulge the hope that this young artist will dwell long and lovingly upon the great classics.

There is no incongruity in hearing the serene beauties of Beethoven interpreted at his youthful hands, there is indeed an added purity and beauty that transports the imagination.

Such a phenomenon is enough to turn the most hear-headed materialist into a confirmed mystic.

One may refer to Yehudi's technical virtues; his broad and well developed tone; his firm and supple bowing; his crisp articulation; his mastery of phrasing; his beautiful intonation; but over and above it all there is the charm of his personality.

Youthful prodigies there have been a plenty, who have startled by their virtuosity, but not within my memory has there emerged another who combines the qualities of musicianship and appeal of personality as manifested in this chubby lad from California.

In the performance of the Concerto, Nikolai Sokoloff and the orchestra gave intimate and well balanced support and there was evident enjoyment in the task of a well-rounded presentation.

Beautifully plastic and euphonious was the playing of the Schubert Symphony, and the deeper note of lamantation was appropriately and expressively communicated through the 'Marcia funebre.'

Geddes Studio photo

ABOUT THE AUTHOR

Frederick Koch, the author, is a resident ASCAP Cleveland composer. He is also the former Director and the Founder of the Koch School of Music, now the Riverside Academy of Music, which he directed from 1971-1988. At this time he left Cleveland to take a position as Editor at International Music Company in New York City. He returned to Cleveland in 1991 and joined the music faculties of Cuyahoga Community College and Baldwin Wallace College.

He has over sixty-five published works in the catalogues of eleven publishers with the majority of his works with Seesaw Music in New York and Southern Music in Texas. His works may be heard on the following record labels: Opus 1, Crystal, Advent, Dimension and most recently Truemedia Records Ltd., of Cleveland.

Koch is a MacDowell Colony Fellow and for four summers he occupied the Composers' Cottage at Wolf Trap Farm Park in Vienna, Virginia. He was awarded the Cleveland Arts Prize in Composition, was first place winner of the Benjamin Award at the Eastman School of Music, and first place winner of the American Choral Directors' Contest. He has received numerous commissions and grants from the National Endowment for the Arts, the American Music Center and ASCAP.

As pianist he appeared as soloist with the National Gallery Orchestra in Washington, D.C. with his Concertino for Piano and Orchestra; with the Cleveland Chamber Symphony with the Bach f minor concerto; with many string quartets; as accompanist for many singers, and in solo recitals.

In addition to his composition and performance activity, Koch's influence as teacher has been felt by many students who are making their way in the world of music.

In 1964 Koch was awarded a plaque by his community for his outstanding contribution to music in the founding of West Shore Concerts which brought the Cleveland Orchestra and Cleveland artists to the West Side and for his co-founding of the Rocky River Chamber Music Society.

Frederick Koch has participated in contemporary forums on the campuses of Hollins College, Virginia; the University of Montevallo, Alabama; Miami University in Oxford, Ohio; Baldwin Wallace College, and Hiram College.

Frederick Koch holds a D.M.A. degree in Composition from the Eastman School of Music, an M.A. in Fine Arts from Case-Western Reserve University, and a B.M. in Piano from the Cleveland Institute of Music. Piano study was with Leonard Shure, Beryl Rubinstein and Arthur Loesser and composition study with Herbert Elwell, Arthur Shepherd, Bernard Rogers and Henry Cowell.

Second Printing 1993

This book has been set
in IBM *Theme* letterface
and *Optima*.
Book design by Ed Fisher, jr.
and portraits by George Mauersberger.
Proofing and art production by
Rae Lou Tickanen and April Cass.
Printed by photo offset in Pittsburgh,
and wire bound in Cleveland.